# An Engineer's Guide *to* Invention and Innovation

**Cawas Phiroze Nazir**

**UNICORN BOOKS**

F-2/16, Ansari Road, Daryaganj, New Delhi-110002
☎ 011-23275434, 23262683, 23250704 • *Fax:* 011-23257790
*E-mail:* info@unicornbooks.in • *Website:* www.unicornbooks.in

**Branch : Mumbai**

23-25, Zaoba Wadi, Thakurdwar, Mumbai-401002
☎ 022-22010941, 022-22053387
*E-mail:* rapidex@bom5.vsnl.net.in

**Showroom :**

★ **PM Publications,** New Delhi
- 10-B, Netaji Subhash Marg, Daryaganj
New Delhi-110002
- 6686, Khari Baoli, Delhi-110006



ISBN 978-81-7806-339-3

*An Engineer's Guide to Invention and Innovation*

**Edition:** 2013



***Printed at :*** Param Offsetters, Okhla, New Delhi-110020

# Preface

In today's competitive world, innovation and creativeness is the key to success. Engineers have a special responsibility towards improving the lives of people by creating solutions to mankind's myriad needs. This book was written for the use of students, practicing engineers and designers in various fields, to show how they could develop their latent creative skills to produce inventive solutions. This well organized book is divided into four parts. The first part has 3 chapters. In chapters 1 to 3 you will find an introductory note covering Engineers and Inventions. Further topics cover the qualities needed to produce useful Inventions, an overview of various techniques used in creative problem solving and a historical background.

Part two covers chapters, 4 through 15. They contain examples of structures and technologies where the problem is defined, the overall concept to arrive at a creative solution is given, the development of the design and the resulting advantages. Examples given cover a variety of engineering fields including civil, structural, architectural, mechanical, renewable energy and aerospace technology.

Part three covers Chapters 16 to 24. They cover products and technologies where innovative solutions led to new and useful improvements for which Complete Specifications were filed to obtain patents. These include products such as bicycles, hot air balloons, concrete piles, human operated watercraft, mill housings and internal combustion engines. Technologies include soft ground tunneling.

Part four covers Chapter 25 and 26. Chapter 25 deals with the Innovation Process that describes the process of effectively planning the technical, marketing and business development of the new technology. Chapter 26 gives the various steps in obtaining a patent.

It is a highly practical book, illustrated throughout by examples drawn from the authors experience working with a multi-disciplinary team of engineers, technologists and scientists in a leading consulting engineering firm. Each case study illustrates briefly how a better solution could be found by examining the root of the problem, looking beyond what most people focus on which can lead to creative alternatives. I am grateful to the many designers, engineers, technologist's and scientist's who have shared their personnel experiences and given their insights and approaches to the subject.

Kolkata **Cawas Phiroze Nazir**
India April 2013

# Acknowledgements

My thanks to managers and colleagues at M.N.Dastur & Co. Ltd. Kolkata from whom I have personally learned ideas, insights, points of view and knowledge through their challenging questions and interesting comments,

Many books listed in the bibliography have provided guidance and good background material for the chapters on invention and creativity. In particular, Thrings 'How to Invent' and J. Jeffery Rawlinsons 'Creative Thinking and Brainstorming' are gratefully acknowledged.

Relatives, close friends and acquaintances for their support. To Phiroze Nazir and Mehroo Nazir, my parents who taught me far more than I used to realize. As always my sons, Anosh, Zubin and Polard who have been sources of inspiration, my wife for her love, patience and understanding.

# Author Profile

NAZIR, CAWAS PHIROZE, civil engineer; b Nagpur Dec 1939, B. E. (Civil ) 1959, M. Eng. (Sheffield Univ) 1962; Asst.Eng Shapoorji Pallonji & Co Mumbai, 1959-1960; asst structural engineer Sheffield City Architects Dept U.K.; tech dir M.N.Dastur & Co Ltd Kolkata, 1963-1999; Consulting engr to date; deputed to foreign Consulting eng. firms in W. Germany and USSR ; Member Indian Stds Instn, Contbr articles to national and international journals; Recepient of 3 gold medals and best paper awards; Fellow Inst. Engrs India, Former mem Inst Civil Engrs U K , Indian Conc Inst. Achievements include patents for rapid underground tunneling technique, concrete auger pile, prestressed concrete mill housing, bi-powered bicycle, birobic bike, other patents registered include manually operated propulsion device for watercraft, solar powered hot air balloon, pedal dive mechanism for bicycles, improved piston and cylinder lining assembly for IC engines. Biography included in Marquis Who's who in Science and Engineering publishers of Who's Who in America. Avocations: cricket, swimming, bicycling, reading.

# Illustrations Credits

General acknowledgement is made to the following for permission to reproduce illustrative material:

1. Fig. 1.1 Board and solid object With permission from Gower Publishing
2. Fig. 4.1 With permission from Jrn of Struc Eng., ASCE Nov 19 86
3. Fig. 4.2 With permission from Jrn of Struc Eng., ASCE Nov 19 86
4. Fig. 4.3 With permission from Jrn of Struc Eng., ASCE Nov 19 86
5. Fig. 6.1 Courtesy Jrn of IEI Jan 1984
6. Fig. 6.2 Courtesy Jrn of IEI Jan 1984
7. Fig. 7.1 Courtesy Jrn. of IEI Sep 1985
8. Fig. 7.2 Courtesy Jrn. of IEI Sep 1985
9. Fig. 8.1 Courtesy Proc. of IABSE Aug 1999
10. Fig. 8.2 Courtesy Proc. of IABSE Aug 1999
11. Fig. 8.3 Courtesy Proc. of IABSE Aug 1999
12. Fig. 9.1 Courtesy Jrn. of IEI May 2003
13. Fig. 9.2 Courtesy Jrn. of IEI May 2003
14. Fig. 9.3 Courtesy Jrn. of IEI May 2003
15. Fig. 10.1 Courtesy Jrn. of IEI Oct 2003

16. Fig.10.2 Courtesy Jrn. of IEI Oct 2003
17. Fig.10.3 Courtesy Jrn. of IEI Oct 2003
18. Fig.11.1 Courtesy Jrn. of IEI Feb 1989
19. Fig. 11.2 Courtesy Jrn. of IEI Feb 1989
20. Fig. 11.3 Courtesy Jrn. of IEI Feb 1989
21. Fig. 12.1 Courtesy Jrn. of IEI May 2005
22. Fig. 13.1 Courtesy Virgin Earth Challenge Mar 2007
23. Fig. 13.2 Courtesy Virgin Earth Challenge Mar 2007
24. Fig. 14.1 Courtesy Jrn. of IEI Nov 2010
25. Fig. 14.2 Courtesy Jrn. of IEI Nov 2010
26. Fig. 15.1 Courtesy Patent Office, Govt. of India Apr 1993
27. Fig. 15.2 Courtesy Patent Office, Govt. of India Apr 1993
28. Fig. 16.1 Courtesy Patent Office, Govt. of India Jun 1999
29. Fig. 16.2 Courtesy Patent Office, Govt. of India Jun 1999
30. Fig. 17.1 Courtesy Patent Office, Govt. of India Jun 1979
31. Fig. 18.1 Courtesy Patent Office, Govt. of India Jun 2005
32. Fig. 18.2 Courtesy Patent Office, Govt. of India Jun 2005
33. Fig. 19.1 Courtesy Patent Office, Govt. of India Mar 1999
34. Fig. 20.1 Courtesy Patent Office, Govt. of India
35. Fig. 20.2 Courtesy Patent Office, Govt. of India
36. Fig. 21.1 Courtesy Patent Office, Govt. of India
37. Fig. 21.2 Courtesy Patent Office, Govt. of India
38. Fig. 21.3 Courtesy Patent Office, Govt. of India
39. Fig.22.1 Courtesy Patent Office, Govt. of India
40. Fig. 22.2 Courtesy Patent Office, Govt. of India
41. Fig. 23.1 Courtesy Patent Office, Govt. of India
42. Fig. 23.2 Courtesy Patent Office, Govt. of India
43. Fig.24.1 Courtesy Tiwari R. et al 'Innovation via Global Route'

# *Contents*

## PART-III



## PART-IV

# Part One

"Human subtlety will never devise an invention more simple or more direct than does nature because in its inventions nothing is lacking, and nothing is superfluous."

**Leonardo da Vinci**

In chapters 1 to 3 you will find an introductory note covering Engineers and Inventions. Further topics cover the outstanding qualities needed to produce useful Inventions, an overview of various techniques used in creative problem solving and a historical background.

# Chapter 1

# Introduction

Most engineers work is founded on solid mathematics and mechanical foundations; however, particularly during conceptual design process, more primal decision making mechanisms such as feeling, intuition, insight and commonsense also take place. They are not learned as much in school as in the everyday life. Experienced engineers find during their professional life that certain problems present themselves that require radical solutions needing creative thought processes. Creative techniques lead to new inventions and designs. It may be said that invention and design are a continuum; at one extreme are acts of invention that are so novel that they seem like a major leap, and, on the other, are incremental changes in design that are tightly constrained by specifications. In between is a large grey area that shades into invention.

## DEFINITION OF INVENTION

An invention is a result of creative act. It is the conception of an idea which can lead to a device to solve a practical human problem in a way which is not an obvious extension of known methods. Inventing a new process or product is certainly a truly creative act just as in the invention of a new hypothesis that makes sense of a group of scientific observations. The example of Archimedes jumping out of his bath and shouting 'Eureka' because he had thought of a way of measuring the volume of the kings crown, and so deciding whether it had the density of copper or gold, is a well known story of an invention to solve a practical problem by applying it to a hitherto unconnected scientific observation. It must be mentioned though that his clear understanding of weight and density helped him to realize the implications of the overflowing of water and translate it into an effective way to measure the density of the crown.

Invention is a thinking process largely related to the brain. It is known that the brain has two hemispheres – a right side and a left side, each with two differing functions. The right side of the brain is related to knowledge based thought process, the ability to be creative, to have a vision of the future and help the inventor to start with a strong feeling of desire to produce a better solution to a human need. The left side of the brain has the ability to get the physical aspect of the invention, to get a feeling for the way things work and to visualize devices which can work within the purview of knowledge based on his experiences and training. A true invention requires the complete working together of the two brains of the inventor. As an example consider the board shown in Fig.1.1. It has three holes cut in it. The holes are circular, triangular and square in shape. Imagine if you were asked to describe a solid object which will pass completely through each hole. It would seem that such an object is not possible.

The solution is shown at the bottom of the figure. It requires cutting and shaping a cylinder of wood so that three views are obtained by turning the object. Each view from three different directions at right angles to each other represents a square, a circle and a triangle. The example requires both creative and analytical thinking – creative in seeing the solid object (visualizing it mentally) and analytical in being able to describe it in words.

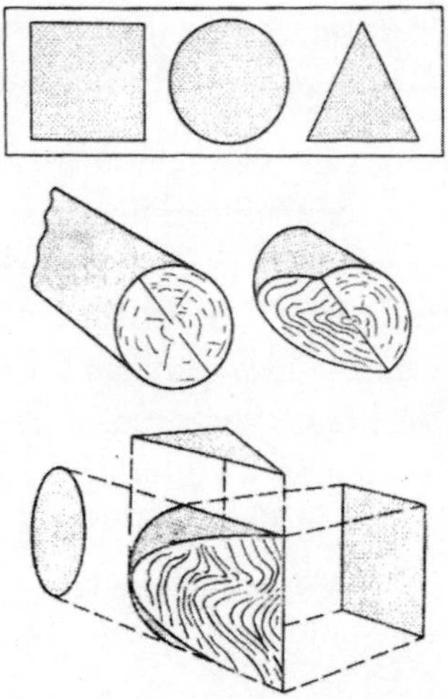

**Fig.1.1**

## CAN AN ENGINEER BE AN INVENTOR

The natural ability to have original inventive ideas is present in most people of normal intelligence. Whenever we solve a small problem which has no obvious logical solution, by finding an unexpected solution, we are inventing. Thus engineers with some spark of originality can be inventors. In fact, the word 'engineer' has its origins from the word 'genius' and 'ingenious' and so directly implying the notion of creativity. Creativity apart, what is even more important is to have the determination of overcoming obstacles to carry the idea past all difficulties, until it is fully realized. This is what Edison meant when he said invention was 90 per cent perspiration and 10 per cent inspiration. In his book *How to Invent*, Thring has stated the following qualities required to be a successful inventor: The first and foremost quality required is unbounded self confidence. The inventor must have faith that he can succeed and is quite determined that he will. This can be done by practising inventing small things like gadgets for one's hobbies or by making it easier to use one's tools in ones home. These help show that the path from the first idea to the final successful realization involves many modifications of the first concept.

The second quality is an emotional one; it is the perseverance and persistence to see the invention pass through every kind of obstacle and opposition, and not to be deterred by repeated failure. A successful inventor will be capable of this if he clearly sees what is a truly valuable idea and then carries it past all difficulties until it is fully realized commercially. There will be times when one comes across serious faults brought about by experimentation or severe constraints in time and money – requiring to end the experimentation. He has to make an honest judgment when to stop, at the same time not allowing his faith in his idea to be destroyed, when the idea is really good.

Third, the inventor needs to develop in himself the intellectual and physical tools necessary to have a workable idea. He must develop the ability to think with the use of well chosen analogues and models and the ability to think with the hands activated so that complex moving systems can be conceived which can work. He must further develop the ability to reflect on every problem back to its first principles. He must visualize the core aspects of his problem he is trying to solve and separate it from the irrelevent details, lest the problem should be made unduly complicated and difficult to grasp.

Fourth, the inventor must have a good measure of self knowledge, he has to know what time of day and under what conditions his mind works most creatively; for example, in the middle of the night, or when discussing with others about the problem. All creative people pinpoint periods when they are in their most creative state; where new ideas can flourish in a flood of energy released by enthusiasm. Importantly, he should learn the secret of switching off the critical facility so that new ideas can form without being strangled by objections before they are fully in the mind. This is done by a conscious effort of will. The inventor has to acquire the art of accumulating the necessary emotional energy to be creative. It is this energy that enables one to take positive outlook and not be depressed by negative aspects (such as the seeming impossibility of the problem, or other peoples discouragement). Keeping oneself in good physical shape definitely helps. Practising Yoga and meditation are other sources which help to achieve a creative state.

Finally he must have what is called the inventor's eye. This means he learns to look at every design and construction around him and think Inquisitively why is it done that way or built that way. This applies to buildings, bridges, highways, airports, industrial structures, hydraulic structures, industrial machinery, airplanes and the numerous other activities that are covered under the term engineering. He must question why things are done in such manner as they are? What do they really want to achieve? Could not the objective be obtained in some other way? Any of these questions could lead to an invention.

The inventor who has already decided that something could be done better, then looks at everything with this problem at the back of his mind and some small observation can give the clue to a solution. The classical example of this is James Watt, who wanted to find a better source of power than the windmill or the muscle, when he noticed the power of steam to lift the lid of a kettle.

## PRINCIPLE RULES OF INVENTION

Some of the principles which apply to the act of invention:

- A problem requiring a truly inventive solution looks impossible to everyone except the truly creative inventor. This is mainly due to the fact that problems which can be solved appear to contradict the scientific facts or known properties of materials because they have been wrongly formulated. Thus the first aim of the inventor should be to work on the formulation of the problem and see if he can find a formulation which is not impossible to solve but which still satisfies the real aim.

- One should start with a clearly defined human need and proceed to invent a better solution to it. If one were to start with an interesting human observation and then proceed to develop it into an invention, the results would not be worth it.
- It often happens that there are two or more quite distinct solutions to any open ended problem. These solutions will, in general, have advantages and disadvantages relative to each other. As an example, in the case of roof trusses, many different types of trusses evolved and with each design new improvements were forthcoming till there are more than two hundred designs available. Thus the inventor could look at less successful alternatives to see if he can invent an improvement or suggest a new line for him to explore.
- On some inventions, it is possible that several people will be working on it quite independently and may reach the same result. This corresponding results because the human need was clear to many people and the necessary physical phenomenon and materials were known. For instance, the English inventor Frank Whittle and the German researcher Hans von Obain developed the turbojet airplane engine more or less simultaneously and independently. Petroski (1996).
- A truly inventive idea cannot be subject to budget constraints or time frames. Only big research

laboratories have the means to pursue promising ideas, the development of which would then require careful budgeting and planning.

- The inventor will have frustrating moments during the course of developing his invention. He must carry on, regardless of the inhibiting factors, with renewed enthusiasm. Once past the inventive moment, the idea should not be frozen more rigidly than is absolutely essential to proceed to the next stage. For example, do not bring in economics before the engineering is clear.

❒

# Chapter 2

## Various Steps Leading Upto The Creative Act

The first step in invention would be to decide what one considers worth inventing. It is a good suggestion to jot down new ideas, whenever they crop up, in a notebook. Once these are written down, they remain at the back of your mind. The solutions are found by concentrating on one particular problem at a time. Discussion with fellow workers is also helpful as it leads to useful suggestions and may even lead to other possibilities. No inventor can be sure of having all the necessary field of knowledge for the different disciplines such as mechanical, electrical, electronic, civil structural, architectural etc. One must be prepared to cooperate with, and acknowledge the work of, others who have something valuable to contribute. The whole object must be to produce a good solution to the problem, not to produce one's own private solution.

The second step to be followed when a problem has been chosen is to make a rough guideline of the rules to be followed.

These rules are the answers to the following questions:

- What is one's main objective – Is it to use fewer materials of construction, make something simpler to construct and more durable?
- What are the secondary objectives, e.g. to be as good as the present system in all respects other than the main objective or to cost not more than 20% extra, besides having a durability at least twice as long? What are the limitations to the solution? It is in this field that the original statement may be too restrictive and by seeing if that any of the restrictions can be relaxed, one is most likely to find an original inventive solution to the problem.

The third step in invention is to develop sufficient mental self-discipline with a view to blocking the mind of all negative thoughts, and conceive of a new idea. When one has arrived at a worthwhile idea, one must answer fully all the doubts one has about it, not by suppressing them but by acquiring confidence, that one can find a solution which will get rid of these doubts. To illustrate, the value of perseverance and pursuing the idea through, here is an example from my own experience. The Greek mathematician Pythagoras formulated his well known theorem that, in a right angled triangle, the square described on the hypotenuse, is equal to the sum of the squares described on the sides containing the right angle. The author was intrigued in finding a solution that extended the relation of squares in Pythagoras' theorem to a relation for cubes. After much deliberation and many trials and errors, he came upon a solution. Now known as Nazir's hypothesis, it states that in any quadrilateral having its sides in the proportion of 3:4:5:6, the cube described on the longest side is equal to the sum of the cubes described on the other three sides. Referring to Fig. 2.1, ABCD is a quadrilateral having sides AB, BC, AD, and CD in the ratio of 3:4:5:6, Then, $CD^3 = AB^3 + BC^3 + AD^3$. This can be expressed as: $a^3 = b^3 + c^3 + d^3$ Verifying with values of AB, BC, AD, and CD equal to 3, 4, 5, and 6 respectively. We have: $6^3 = 5^3 + 4^3 + 3^3$ or $216 = 125 + 64 + 27$. There are no solutions to the simple variation on Nazir's hypothesis, $a^z + b^z + c^z = d^z$ where a, b, c and d are integers and z is larger than three. The conjecture is somewhat similar to Fermats last Theorem, and is left for others to solve. It may require someone of Andrew Wile's caliber, who solved the Fermat Theorem in 1993 after a gap of about 350 years.

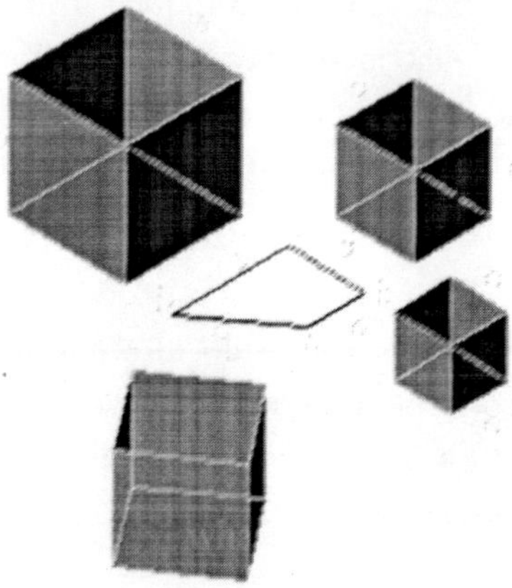

**Fig. 2.1**

## THE MOMENT OF INSIGHT- THE CREATIVE ACT

There are various methods used by inventors to achieve the moment of inspiration.

The first consists of setting a time limit and forcing oneself to maintain close attention to the problem until an idea of a possible solution presents itself.

The second involves shelving the problem temporarily when one cannot see a good solution but for which one feels there is a good solution.

The third method of finding an inventive solution mainly used in organizations is called Brainstorming. (With acknowledgement to J, Rawlinson) It involves getting a large number of ideas from a group of people in a short time. Rawlinson (2002) has defined six basic stages in a brainstorming session. They are as follows:

*State the problem and discuss*. This stage is meant to give people a minimum amount of information about the problem.

*Restate the problem*- In this stage the problem is restated including the words 'How to'

*Select a basic restatement* An agreed upon restatement is selected and then prefaced with the words 'In how many ways can we ....' This prompts participants to ask for solutions.

*Warm-up session*. Basically a session to throw up ideas, the key phrase being 'Other uses for...'

*Brainstorm*. In this stage, a leader reads the restatements and calls for ideas. The purpose is to spark off further ideas from those already generated.

*Wildest Idea* Basically this takes the most foolish idea from the brainstorming session and attempts to turn it around into some more useful idea.

The ideas then generated are evaluated to identify the few good ideas and interpret them.

The fourth method is of Synectics developed by Gordon (1961) Synectics is an idea-generating technique where a group consisting of a leader, a client and about six participants sit together in a room and start a process to solve a problem presented by the client. The process aims at idea development and revolves around three main stages of idea, paraphrase and itemized response These are repeated a number of times until a possible solution is reached.

The synectics process has the distinct advantage of leading

to possible solutions in a very short time. Brainstorming, however, has the advantage in producing a much larger number of ideas, thereby widening the choices, and thereby effecting economies and increasing efficacy.

The fifth technique is 'Attribute Listing'. In this technique the attributes or characteristics of an object are identified and then examined to see whether they can be improved or changed.

The sixth technique is referred to as 'Forced Relationships'. This technique takes two or more unrelated objects or ideas and asks the question: 'If these were combined, what new product could be produced'. Quite often two or more unrelated products can be combined to form a totally new product. Incorporating advantageous aspects of other ideas which have the potential to improve something that is so important that it is worth looking at. As an example, William Le Baron Jenny built the first skyscraper in Chicago. It was ten floors tall, and this height was made possible by using a steel frame. During that time steel frames were already commonly used to support bridges. So Jenny's innovation amounted to transferring from bridges the idea of using a steel structure to support something vertical (a tall building instead of something horizontal (a long bridge).

The seventh technique is referred to as 'Lateral Thinking and PO'. This technique was developed by Dr. Edward de Bono. Creative thinking, as we have seen, is a wide ranging or lateral thought process requiring suspended judgment, and a willingness to bring out new ideas, however silly or wild. Deferring judgment on the idea may, however, lead to other ideas. This, in effect, says to give the idea a chance, because it may lead to other ideas, not so silly, and eventually engenders useful ideas.

The eight technique builds a Check List to question ideas and objects and can result in new ideas being developed. One check list developed by Osborn (1957) has the following headings;

| | | |
|---|---|---|
| Put to other uses? | Substitute? | Adapt? |
| Rearrange? | Modify? | Reverse? |
| Magnify? | Combine? | Minify? |

Another problem solving, analysis and forecasting tool is TRIZ. It was developed by Gerick Altshuller and his colleagues after studying patterns of invention based on observations from thousands of patents. The study found that the vast majority of problems that require inventive solutions typically reflect a need to overcome a trade off between two contradictory elements. The resulting analytical tools were listed as 40 inventive principles that allowed truly inventive solutions. Following this approach the typical solutions can be found by defining the contradictions which need to be resolved systematically – considering which of the 40 principles maybe applied to provide a specific solution which will overcome the contradictions in the problem at hand, enabling a solution that is closer to the ultimate ideal result. As an example, if we want to build a railway freight wagon whose body is not prone to corrosion, we need to build the body from stainless steel or aluminium alloy; but this will increase the cost of the wagon; that is more of something desirable also brings something less desirable. An inventive solution which challenges one to be inventive, must involve several such contradictions. Conventional solutions typically trade-off one contradictory parameter for another; no special inventiveness is needed for that. Rather, the inventor could develop a creative approach for resolving the contradictions such as inventing a wagon body that is more corrosion proof without increasing the cost of the wagon.

## FORMULATING THE IDEA

When the inventor has got a glimpse of a possible solution to the problem, he must proceed carefully to crystallize the idea.

The first thing he must do with the idea is to try to formulate the essence of it, either by a sketch or by writing down a few words as a reminder of the field of knowledge where a solution might lie.

He must view the new idea from all angles before beginning any kind of detailed work. You do not yet concern yourself with any questions of economics, such as reliability, maintenance, cost of the materials of construction, but you do ask can it work, can it be made with existing materials, can it give a better solution to an existing problem?

You ask the primary engineering questions and only if you can formulate the solution in such a way as suggests that you have answered these, do you proceed to the second stage of making approximate calculations and drawings and begin to add details of dimensions, method, optimum materials, and work out static and dynamic forces, stability, and other key factors (process sheet).

It may then be necessary to make models to explore three dimensional relationships. These models may be made of easily worked materials, that have just enough strength to serve their purpose.

## IMPLEMENTING THE IDEA

Once you have created the solution you must be ready to implement it This is a big step forward and there may be doubts. To clear the mind of any uncertainties, gauge your reactions to the questions listed below:

- Is it contrary to known laws of science?
- Can it work in practice and achieve the desired aim?

- Can it be made with known materials and known method of constructions?
- Can it conform to various Codes of Practice?
- Can it be reliable and easily maintained?
- Can it be made reasonably cheaply?
- What are the running costs, labour requirements and maintenance costs?
- How long will it last?
- Could there be a collapse and would it be disastrous?
- Does it solve the problem?

If you have no doubts about the above answers you can proceed to implement your idea and take confidence that you will create an effective solution.

## HANDLING NEGATIVE RESPONSE

However good you may think your creative solution is, there are bound to be critics. As Mark Twain said, "The man with an original idea is a crank until the idea succeeds". Handling criticism will depend on the type of comments offered. If the observation includes information that you have overlooked a shortcoming in the idea, then it is best to eliminate that flaw. Another criticism leveled against you may point out disadvantages stemming from your idea under review, while, you know that your idea does not have. This misunderstanding could be because the critic has not completely understood your idea and may be best resolved by explaining your idea more coherently. Yet another form of criticism conveys a negative opinion without indicating whether it is valid or not. This may best be countered by asking specific questions as to what aspect of the idea is found wanting in this, and thus determine if his criticism is really valid. Remember that even if you have created a solution that in fact does offer benefits, other people may not share your confidence that the invention or innovation will work. History abounds in such examples, a few of which are listed below:

The electric bulb was dismissed by the British Parliamentary Committee, which said " ... good enough for our transatlantic friends... but unworthy of the attention of practical or scientific men".(1878);

The railway builders in the early nineteenth century were advised that speeds of 50 m.p.h. would cause nose bleeds, and that trains could not go through tunnels because people would get asphyxiated;

In 1889 Thomas Alva Edison referring to Nikola Tesla's 'AC' mentioned, " Fooling around with alternating current is just a waste of time. Nobody will use it, ever";

In 1933, Lord Rutherford said, " the energy produced by breaking down the atom is a poor kind of thing. Anyone who expects a source of power from transformation of these atoms is talking moonshine";

In 1962, Dennis Gabor, Nobel prize winning scientist failed to anticipate e-mail and the modem. He commented that " Transmission of documents via telephone wires is possible, in principle, but the apparatus required is so expensive that it will never become a practical solution";

In 1899, the Literary Digest commented that " the horseless carriage is at present a luxury for the wealthy; and although its price will probably fall in the future, yet it will never, of course, come into as common use.

Such statements from prominent people may discourage others from trying new and unusual ideas, particularly if the idea is radically different from common practice. Creative persons should not be deterred from criticism and be prepared to take risks if they are to lead the way in developing new inventions and technologies. Rewards and acclamation will follow later when the ideas are found to be practical and beneficial.

Despite the fact that engineers everywhere have an innate ability to be creative, third world countries are not doing enough to harness invention and creative thoughts, and in some cases tend to stifle innovation and creativity outright. This is typically due to a combination of factors: insufficient financial resources, inadequate number of role models, educational systems that don't inspire or value creativity, and social/political environments which are not conducive to creativity, invention and innovation.

❒

# Chapter 3

## Historical Background

The very great names we use to describe the great epochs of the past–the Stone Age, the Bronze Age, and the Iron age–tells us that invention is the essence of civilization. Mankind's programme of improvements have been erratic and unpredictable. But good ideas are rarely forgotten. They are borrowed and copied and spread more widely, in an accelerating process which make the luxurious of one age the necessities of the next.

Perhaps, the first time ideas worthy of the name of invention, even though invented in many different places, are the eye of the needle and the string of a bow.

**Needle and thread:** Stone age people stitched their skin garments together with thread or tendons. In each skin they bore a hole and then passed the hook of the head through it. The development of the bone or ivory needle, with an eye, speeded up the process immeasurably Needles of this kind have been found in caves in Europe from the late Paleolithic period about 15,000 years ago.

**Bow and arrow:** The sudden release of stored energy when a forcibly bent strip of wood is allowed to snap back into its natural shape, is more rapid and more powerful than any impulse of which human muscles are capable; yet human muscles at a slower pace have the strength to bend the strip of wood. This principle of bow was discovered about 15,000 years ago. Bows and arrows have been made available at the disposal of the human power right from that time.

Today, we stand on the shoulders of a thousand generation of inventors. Although the examples that follow are hardly comprehensive, yet they are few noteworthy stopovers on the road to innovation.

**Notable Engineers and Inventors whose biographies appear in various books:**

**Leonardo da Vinci** (1452-1519), was a celebrated Italian Renaissance architect, inventor, engineer, sculptor and painter. His sketches revealed inventions that included an innovative clock, a spring driven vehicle, an armoured car, a parachute, a crude helicopter, and many other flying machines to name a few.

**Alfred B. Nobel** (1833-1896). Swedish chemist and engineer who invented dynamite. Made millions from his invention and left his fortune to establish the Nobel Prize, worldwide.

**Isambard Kingdom Brunel** (1801-1859) Extravagance of Brunel's creations set standards for the next generation of engineers to follow. Most prominent work include, inter alia. Great Western railway connecting London and Bristol was a clever achievement that avoided steep gradients, by using a network of low rise bridges and tunnels.

**Thomas Telford** (1757-1834) Father figure of civil engineering profession. Built 1,000 miles of roads, 1,200 bridges, including the Mennai Suspension Bridge. He improved the method of building roads with broken stones by analyzing stone thickness, road traffic, road alignment and gradient slopes. Eventually his design became the norm for all roads everywhere. He was the first President of The Institution of Civil Engineers, U.K .from 1820-1834.

**Eugene Freyssinet** (1879- 1962). Received patent for the invention of the jacked arch technique used for the first time for the bridge at Chatel-de. His name is primarily linked, however, with prestressed concrete, which he invented, using prestressed concrete steel wire (which was allowed to be drawn by passing through wire drawing diamonds) and further persisted with and developed into a highly competitive and notable form of construction.

**Karl Terzaghi** (1883- 1963), The modern science of soil mechanics is a discipline that he established and developed. Modern virtuosity in handling soils and designing massive heavy foundations with confidence and safety developed directly from his basic contribution.

**Andre Coyne** (1891-1960) French, was the greatest designer of arch dams. Some of his notable works include the Kariba Dam and the Daniel Johnson Dam.

**Richard Buckminster Fuller** (1895-1983). Fuller became famous for his huge geodesic dome, which can be seen as part of military radar stations, city halls and exhibition attractions. Their construction is based on extending basic principles to build simple tensegrity structures. After getting his first patent on domes in 1954, Fuller went on to explore the natures own constructing principles to find solutions for designs in many areas of human life. Fuller contributed a wide range of ideas, designs and inventions to the world, particularly in the areas of practical inexpensive shelters and transportation.

**Washington Roebling** (1837- 1921), a US civil engineer best known for his work on the Brooklyn Bridge, originally started by his father John A. Roebling.

**Stephan Timoshenko** (1878-1972), is reputed to be the father of modern engineering mechanics. He wrote many of the seminal works in the areas of engineering mechanics and strength of materials.

**Fazlur R. Khan** ( born 1929) designer of the Sears Tower, John Hancock Center and One Shell Plaza. He was the first designer to replace the traditional steel skeleton of beams and columns with the tubular concept in which the exterior framing resists wind loads.

**Nikola Tesla** – prolific inventor who invented various kinds of alternating current (AC) electric motors, high voltage transformers, devices for distributing AC electric power, various kinds of neon and fluorescent lamps and many other inventions , only a few of which he patented.

❑

# Part Two

## Innovative Engineering Solutions

"O! for a muse of fire, that would ascend the brightest heaven of invention."

**William Shakespeare**

The following chapters, 4 through 15, contain examples of structures and technologies where the problem is defined, the overall concept to arrive at a creative solution is given, concrete shape in the form of design is reached, and concludes with advantages. The examples cover a variety of engineering fields including civil, structural, mechanical, energy and aeronautical.

# Chapter 4

# Multispan Balanced Suspension Bridge

In an ever shrinking world, it has become necessary to have increasing number of permanent crossings between nations and regions separated by a large body of water. These permanent crossings are provided in the nature of tunnel or bridge systems and are superb engineering feats, Some examples are: the 38km long Pontchartrain Bridge: 8.85 km long Lake Maracaibo Bridge and the 53.58km long Sei Kan Rail Tunnel.

For very long crossings, above ground solutions are generally preferred. They are aesthetically pleasing, and more importantly long stretches of submerged tunnels pose serious maintenance and ventilation problems. Bridge types considered economical for long stretches are the multispan cable- stayed bridge with navigation spans up to 500m or a suspension bridge of longer central span used in conjunction with a number of smaller flanking spans (see Fig 4.1.) Both these suspended structures have certain limitations. One by its range of span and the other by its need for massive anchorages. Important sea lanes such as the English Channel or the Straits of Gibraltar can no longer be restricted by bridge types having such limitations. Thus there was a need for a new class of bridge system that could provide large spans over long stretches of water. The Balanced Multispan Suspension Bridge system was developed to fill this need. Nazir (1986)

Fig. 4.1

## OVERALL CONCEPT

The great majority of suspension bridges are made with cable supporting in three spans. With the long spans being limited by the strength and weight of the cable, some of the longer spans have simply consisted of several three- span bridges placed end to end as found in the west bay crossing of the San Francisco Oakland bay Bridge. Here a conventional suspension bridge is present on each side of a central anchor pier. These anchorages are massive structures and in no way enhance the beauty of the bridge. Another problem to be overcome was the flexibility of the pylons with traffic load in one span only. The configuration developed (Fig.4.2) has the following salient features:

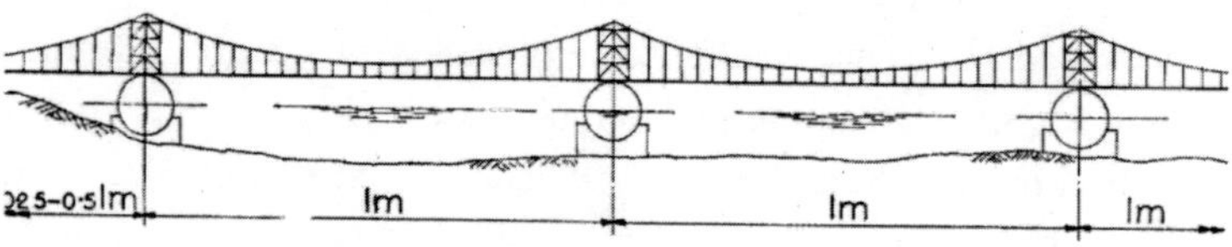


Fig.4.2

- It has a number of main spans and two end spans. All the spans are of equal length, ensuring that the dead load on each side of the tower are balanced.

- The cables of each span are anchored to the tower.
- The four legged towers are provided with a bracing system, which significantly increases its bending stiffness. The pier is in the form of a hollow walled reinforced concrete cylinder. The circular form is ideal for transferring the loads in axial compression. (Fig.4.3).
- A concrete saddle supports the pier and helps in transmitting the forces from the pier to the sea bed.

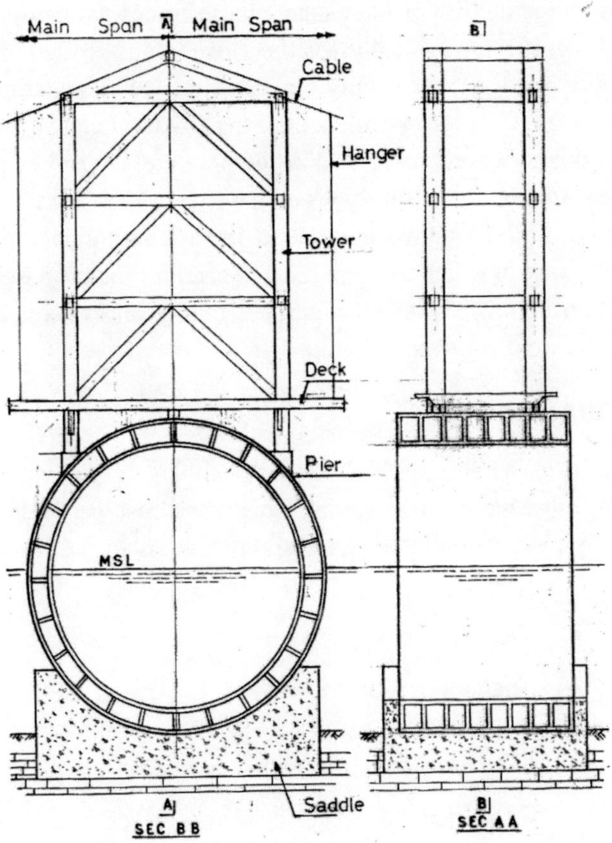


Fig.4.3

## DESIGN

The design philosophy was aimed at keeping unbalanced forces on the tower and pier to a minimum. Each cable from an adjacent span is anchored to the tower top. The reaction of the cable force at the tower induces vertical and horizontal forces in the tower frame. As the adjacent spans are equal, the system is in equilibrium under dead load conditions. Similarly, at the pier level, the forces from the tower legs are balanced by the reactions from the pier saddle. Unbalanced forces on the tower do occur due to live load, wind and temperature. For long spans, these forces are comparatively less significant. Typically for the Bosphorous Bridge, the cable tension for live load is only 6 per cent of the value indicated for dead load. Of more importance are the environmental loads on the pier due to wave, current, tides, temperature, ice and earthquake. These forces are resisted by its own weight plus the fixity provided by the saddle. A study was made to obtain a preliminary indication of the way in which the quantities of steel for the proposed bridge system compare with conventional multispan systems, and the results were very encouraging.

## ADVANTAGES

- The use of high strength cables in tension leads to economy in material, weight and cost, particularly if the self weight becomes significant, as in the case of long spans.
- The use of costly anchoring piers is avoided.
- The application of braced towers gives the system excellent stiffness properties, thus permitting multispans to be used.
- Repetition of spans lead to an optimal saving in construction cost and time.

- As the cables are directly anchored to the tower top, instead of being laid over a saddle as in a conventional suspension bridge, there is no bending stress reduction to be made for the curved cable.
- The system permits of balancing enormous opposing dead load forces from adjoining spans leaving only unbalanced live load forces to be transmitted to the substructure.
- Improved stiffness makes the structure less prone to aerodynamic instability.
- The circular pier not only provides a wide base for the tower legs but also assists in reducing the tower height.
- The cellular wall of pier provides adequate floating capacity and use of straightforward ballasting technique for submerging the unit.
- The complete bridge system is elegant and neatly expresses its function.

❐

# Chapter 5

# Ground Improvement Technique Through Shock Wave Propogation

The rapid expansion of population and prosperity in developing countries has resulted in a scarcity of suitable land for development. Hence, poor ground is being increasingly brought into use requiring greater attention to the design and construction of foundations. As piling could be a very expensive proposition for such sites, the focus has been on developing new techniques such as vibrofloatation , dynamic consolidation etc. to improve the strength of such soils. With new techniques being developed which enabled the behaviour of impacted soil to be predicted with sufficient accuracy, it became possible to introduce another method of soil stabilization using controlled blasting.

## OVERALL CONCEPT

Most soil stabilization methods depend on compaction, whereby an increase in the density of the soil is obtained by packing of soil particles using mechanical means. Some of the methods used are (a) Preloading, which consists of applying surcharge load, so as to induce settlements of the ground before the structure is built; (b) Sand drains and sand wicks which introduce drainage channel in the soil to dissipate the pore water pressure and accelerate consolidation; (c).Dynamic consolidation which improves the strength of the ground by repeated application of high energy impacts to the ground surface; (d) Vibrofloatation and vibrocompaction which uses a vibrofloat to induce vibrations in a loosely packed soil that gets densified due to elimination of interangular friction; and (e) Stone columns which are formed in the ground by vibrodisplacement or other means and are used to support footings directly. The proposed method Nazir (1981), uses vibration induced by explosives as a means of soil compaction The vibrations setup when an explosive is detonated, reduce voids present in both naturally formed and filled ground, leading to an improvement in the load bearing capacity and shear strength of the ground.

## DESIGN

The aim of controlled blasting is to ensure that the total energy released by blasting is absorbed by the soil. Explosives used for primary blasting may be grouped into three categories: (a) conventional high explosives, such as gelignite, dynamite and trimonite; (b) factory mixed blasting agents, such as nobelite, and (c) compositions mixed on site, ammonium nitrate and fuel oil being the most common. When an explosive in a drill hole is detonated, it is transformed into gas. The large energy released creates a pressure wave around the hole. The energy impact of the blast producing these waves causes consolidation in saturated soils by partial liquefaction, and instant and dramatic increase in permeability and the creation of tension cracks. These assist percolation of the pore water accompanied by ground settlement and consequential increase in bearing capacity. The quantity of explosives required is difficult to estimate, since it depends upon the effects of local geology, soil condition and the structural damage associated with ground motions. Information gained from detonating trial charges in a controlled area is vital to the efficiency, economy and safety of the subsequent programmes.

## ADVANTAGES

- Increase in bearing capacity for clays by 100% to 300%, silty sands upto 400% and sand and gravels 200% to 400%.
- Because of the uniformity of compaction achieved through continous site monitoring and control, future differential settlements can be kept well within the specified limits.
- Optimum reduction of time compared with other consolidation methods, resulting in reducing contract duration. .
- In most cases, this treatment would be more economical than other conventional systems (piling, excavation and backfilling, static preloading, vibro-flotation etc.).
- It is adaptable to most kinds of soil encountered in constructional work and may even be used for land fills such as domestic and industrial wastes, which may not even be considered suitable foundation for construction.

❐

# Chapter 6

# An Earth Balanced Cantilever Bridge

Bridges have always figured prominently in human history. They are monuments to man's indomitable will to explore and go beyond the immediate confines of his dwelling. Bridge building is, no doubt, expensive and time-consuming but an inevitable recessity for any country profoundly concerned with expanding its network of roads and railways to serve uninterrupted the essential needs of agriculture, industry and defense. Thus bridge building has been a constant challenge to the ingenuity and perseverance of the designer to develop bridge types that will successfully fulfill the structural, functional, and other requirements at a given location, for the least amount of expenditure. This has prompted a new type of bridge, called "Earth Balanced Cantilever Bridge" to be developed Nazir (1984). By making ingenuous use of the passive earth pressure behind the retaining wall to balance the super structure loads a new design has been created which proportions the structure for more efficient utilization of material.

**Overall Concept** The structural arrangement of small and medium span bridges comprises a deck which supports the live loads and the abutment walls which support the end spans of the superstructure, and retains the filling of the embankment at the rear. This earth filling, besides producing active pressure on the wall, also provides a potential abutting force in the form of passive resistance. This led to the realization that if this force could somehow be utilized to balance the loads from the superstructure, a very economical design would result. The manner in which this is sought to be achieved is shown in Fig.6.1.

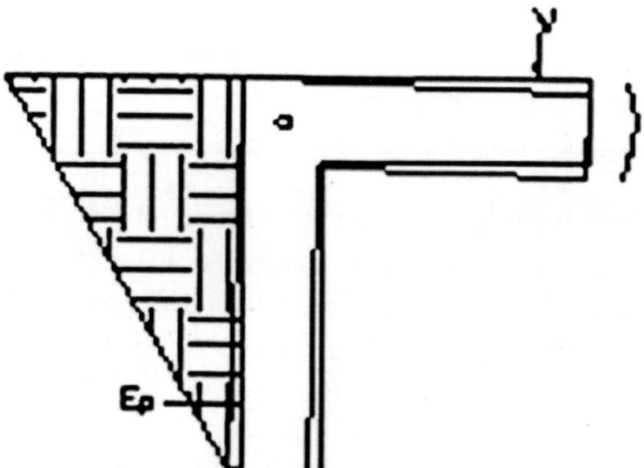


Fig.6.1

The two arms (representing the deck and the breast wall) are rigidly connected and are supported at the corners on two horizontal trunnions upon which it can be made to rotate in a vertical plane. The overturning moment of the superstructure about the pivot point is balanced by the moment of the passive force developed about the same axis. This concept has been used to develop the earth balanced cantilever bridge see Fig.6.2

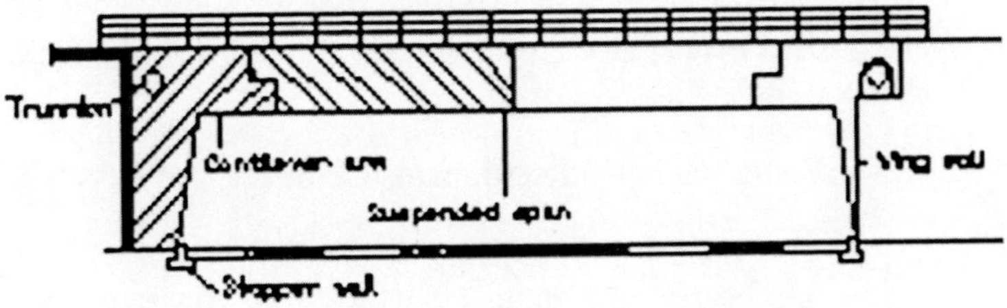


Fig.6.2

## DESIGN

The design commences with the selection of the structural arrangement. For medium span bridges a suspended span resting on two cantilever frames is adapted: Determination of the span lengths and dimensions of the super structure and substructure: Calculation of the dead and live load moments about the pivotal axis: Calculation of active and passive earth pressures and their corresponding moments about the pivotal axis: Checking stability of structure due to overturning moments of imposed loads against balancing moments from passive earth pressure force: Determination of deflection for various load combinations: Proportioning size of structural members: Determination of bearing sizes: Determination of section for wing wall due to load from bearing and earth pressure: The main stages of construction involve; constructing wing walls; constructing vertical and horizontal arms and suspending from bearings on wing walls; jacking up horizontal arm to allow for downward movement due to vertical loads; backfilling; and constructing suspended arm.

## ADVANTAGES

- The bridge has an improved depth over span ratio. This is particularly useful in case of over bridges where the headroom available is generally restricted.

- The proportion of material used for construction such as concrete, steel, formwork etc. are much less, resulting in reduced costs.
- Being statically determinate, the design is much simpler.
- The design can be adapted to suit bridges of steel, reinforced concrete, prestressed concrete or a combination thereof.
- Reduced embankment heights lead to further savings in costs.
- The design permits use of precast supported spans. This is, decidedly, advantageous where it is not possible to provide formwork for the entire deck or where differential settlement is anticipated precluding continuous structures.

❒

# Chapter 7

## Novel Low Cost Housing

From the very dawn of history people's need for enclosures has remained almost indispensable. Houses are peoples physical shelter from natures inclemency and should be safe and comfortable. In developing countries, the major need for decent low cost housing is in the rural regions since the large proportion of the population live in the countryside. In these regions, what is critical is the availability of resources. The latter being limited, it becomes necessary to stretch the available resources to the maximum extent possible. In this context, economy in building construction assumes special significance. Hence, there is a need for alternative construction systems in which less materials (even alternative materials) are utilized in conformity with the principles of Value Engineering; and in which the local inhabitants can use their own personal effort in erecting their houses with a minimum of training and supervision. This has prompted a new design for a novel low cost single storey house Nazir (1985). See Fig.7.1.

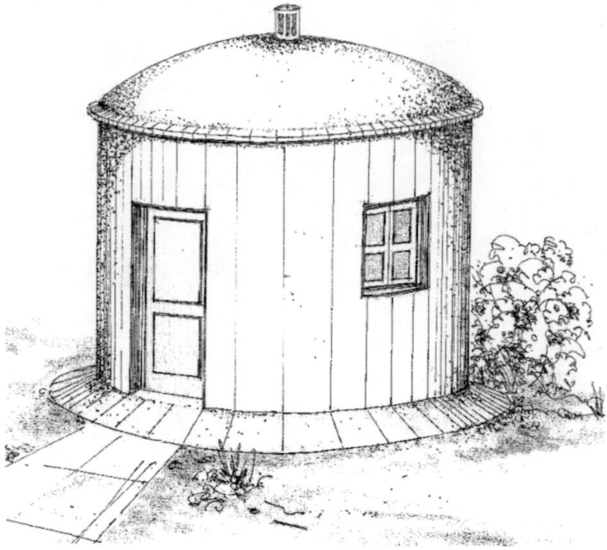

Fig. 7.1

## OVERALL CONCEPT

The modern trend in developing lower cost housing has been influenced by shortage of important building material such as cement and bricks and the increasingly high value materials like steel. This has resulted in construction systems in which less materials are utilized. Many types of cheap housing have been developed using precast roofing systems and composite walls of burnt and unburnt bricks. Pursuing waste utilization principles, and serving the cause of environmental management; fly-ash, emanating as waste in thermal/coal power plants, is increasingly utilized in the making of bricks and further in the manufacture of 'Pozzlana' cament which is used as a substitute for the 'Portland cement'. Other types include funicular shells, jack arches with R.C.C. beams, reinforced brickwork, stone slab on timber beams and joists, and corrugated roof sheeting. The present concept developed from the following considerations:

- Single storey would suffice, since adequate land is available for horizontal level construction, as is the case in most rural areas.
- Reduced construction costs could be achieved adopting new design for roof and walls, which together constitute about 65% of the total cost of construction.

## DESIGN

The proposed design is shown in Fig.7.2. The layout is circular in plan having an internal diameter of 3.8m. It has a floor area of 11.33 sqm. and a plinth area of approximately 14.25 sqm. The concrete roof is of segmental dome construction . The concept of dome is attractive as it offers the most for the least. The central angle of the dome is kept in such a way as the shell is in compression in both meridional and radial directions. This permits the dome being built with a minimum concrete thickness and nominal reinforcement. A cowl is provided at the top of the roof for ventilation. Inflatable fabric has been suggested for the formwork, keeping in mind the multiple use and ease of transportation. The superstructure is of brick diaphragm wall construction having an overall width of approximately 230 mm (depending on size of bricks). The wall is treated as a box section and thus offers greater rigidity, at the same time, providing an excellent insulation barrier. Openings are provided in the wall for a door and a window. The loads to be transmitted to the soil are very light and open foundations with spread footings would normally be sufficient The main stages of construction involve: levelling 5m x 5m plots of land; excavating a circular trench 750 mm wide and 750 mm deep; building foundation brickwork up to 300mm above ground level; building 2.5m high and 230 mm width diaphragm wall in cement lime mortar(1:1:6); placing and inflating inflatable membrane for roof; putting reinforcement and casting roof with concrete grade M15; deflating and removing membrane; completing flooring with a base of lime concrete over which a layer of unburnt bricks is placed; plastering walls with a 12 mm thick coat of plaster (1 lime:1 surkhi:1 sand); fitting of door and window.

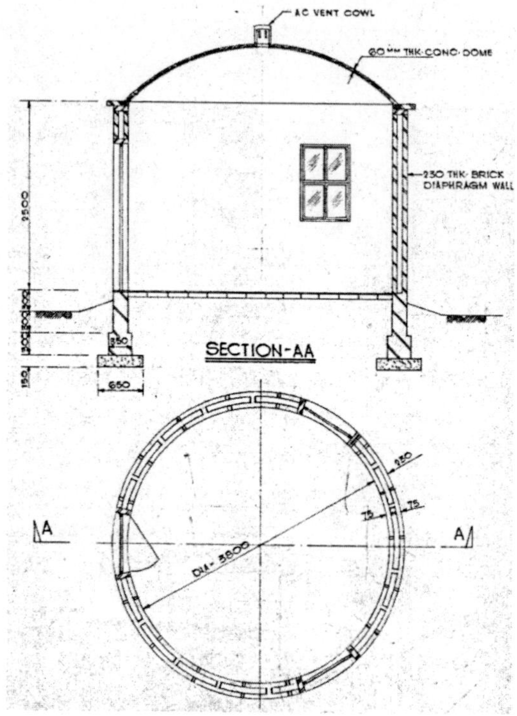


Fig.7.2

## ADVANTAGES:

- As the house is built of sound building materials, it is durable, watertight and fire resistant.
- Thermal comfort is substantially improved by the hollow walls and domed roof.
- Practically, maintenance free.
- Design is adaptable to various sites.

- Has few components and can be built with simple equipment.
- Circular shape helps in resisting large wind forces.
- Simple construction techniques that can be successfully used by unskilled people with a minimum of training and supervision.
- Requirements of building materials such as bricks, cement and reinforcement is reduced, thus substantially lowering construction costs.

❐

# Chapter 8

## Prestressed Aluminium Arch Dam

Dams are effective water retaining structures, and this feature has been advantageously utilized for the benefit of man and his economic activity. Dams have been built from various materials. However, concrete and embankment dams seem to be predominent because of the simplicity of their design and construction. With a view to reducing the large volumes of materials used, and to take advantage of the topography of the site, arch dams have been developed. These dams are curvilinear in plan and resist the horizontal loads by shell action. Thus the strength of the material is more fully developed. In a bid to further optimize the arch profile a new type of dam called the Prestresed Aluminium Arch Dam has been proposed Nazir (1999).

### OVERALL CONCEPT

The arch dam carries its load by compression. Ideally, the more logical way of containing any liquid is by tension members. It has been shown that it is more efficient in material to carry a force in tension than compression and bending. However, since rock is generally weak in tension, it was decided to use a structural system which would take advantage of the tensile membrane action yet load the foundation in an optimal manner in compression for the hydraulic load. This was hoped to be achieved by constructing the wall of a conventional arch dam from material having high tensile strength and then prestressing it so that stresses opposite to those originating from hydrostatic load are produced.

## DESIGN

The new design for the prestressed aluminium arch dam is shown in Fig.8.1.

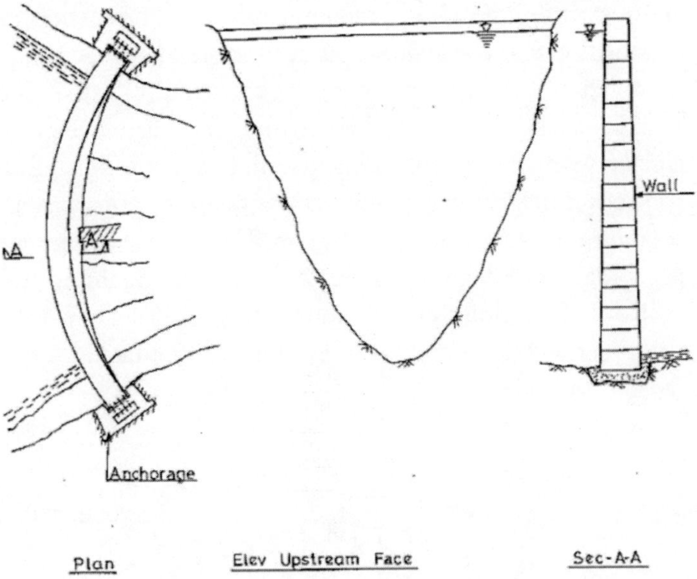


**Fig.8.1**

The main wall is a multi-cellular box structure made from structural aluminium alloy and having a parabolic profile, with its convex side facing head water and its ends fixed to anchorages within the rock embankment. The wedge shaped reinforced concrete anchorage blocks are embedded in the rock face to which the wall of the dam is anchored by pretensioned anchor bolts. For the new design, a parabolic profile of the arch was selected, as this results in an economical structure for loading which is predominantly uniformly distributed. To reduce the maximum stresses on the arch under hydrostatic load, the arch was prestressed during the reservoir empty condition in a manner so as to induce tensile stresses throughout the arch section. As seen from Fig 8.2, the arch can be visualized as a tensile arch tensioned by a prestressing force 'P' which is equivalent to loading the arch by a uniformly distributed load q. In the final stage, when the reservoir is full the structure is designed as a conventional arch and resists uniform load predominantly by compression in the member Fig 8.3. The main stages in construction would comprise: (a) diverting the river; (b) laying out the dam; (c) excavation for foundation and anchorages; (d) constructing concrete foundations and anchorage; (e) fabricating aluminium alloy box girder in panels and transporting to site; (f) erecting box girder panels and welding them together; (g) temporarily securing box girders to anchorages with high tensile bolts; (h) tensioning the bolts from each end of the girder simultaneously; (j) sealing the joint between the girder and anchorage; (k) installing service facilities such as ladders, manholes etc.

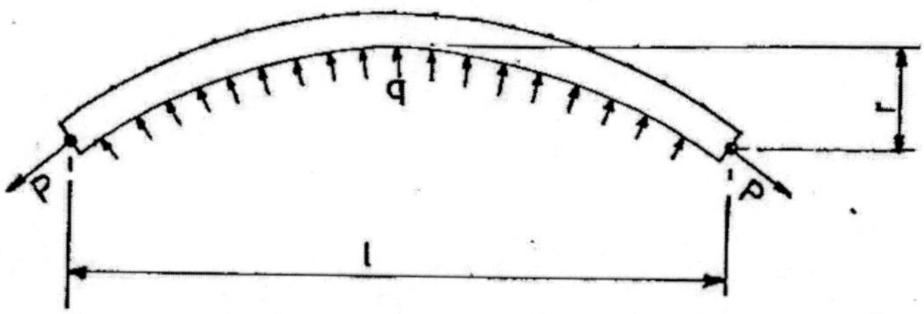


Fig.8.2

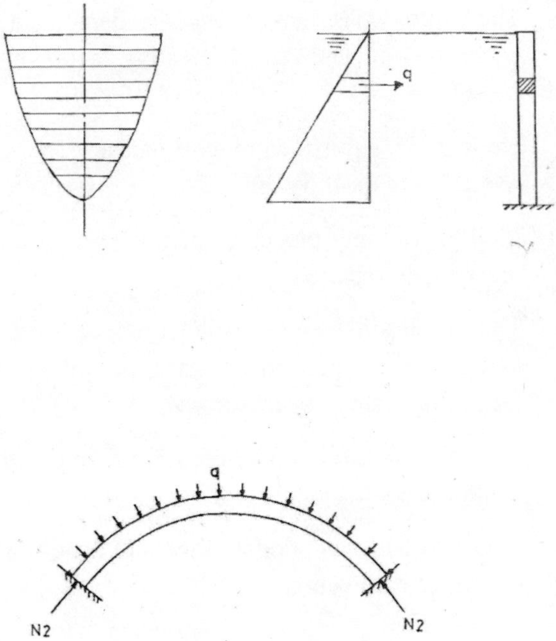


Fig.8.3

## ADVANTAGES

- The use of aluminium alloy and HT bolts offers a much higher strength to weight ratio leading to significant advantages in transportation, handling, and load bearing capacity.
- Prestressing of aluminium wall permits balancing of water load leading to a more economical design.
- Repetition of multi-cellular boxes forming the body of the dam leads to an optimal saving in construction costs and time.
- The wall is free from corrosion and hence maintenance costs are greatly reduced.

- The hollow passages within the dam, lead to better conditions of heat release creating favourable thermal conditions.
- Savings in sub-structure cost because of substantial reduction of dead weight.
- Modern welding processes permit leaking joints to be more easily repaired.
- The cavities in the multi-cellular box construction serve as excellent inspection galleries, permitting the entire face of the dam to be monitored.
- The parabolic arch profile permits of a more gentle arch abutment conjugation.
- The dam has exceptional grace and beauty and neatly expresses its function.

❐

# Chapter 9

## Prestressed Steel Arch Bridge

Using arch form to span deep gorges with steep rocky banks is not new. However, in recent times other types of construction due to high costs of formwork and construction have eclipsed the arch bridge. This has prompted a new bridge system being proposed called the Prestressed Steel Arch Bridge, Nazir (2003). Its main load bearing members are steel arch ribs that are prestressed with high tensile rock anchors embedded in the banks. The prestressing aims to achieve material economy by relieving the arch rib bending moments induced under self-weight and non uniform load. The principle design criteria are design of arch ribs as tensile arch under prestressing load during self weight condition and as a conventional arch under live load and temperature variation.

### OVERALL CONCEPT

The arch bridge carries its load by compression and this makes concrete an ideal material of construction. However, high costs of formwork and construction time have restricted their use. Thus, steel has been chosen as the principal construction material.

To make the design more cost effective, the main arch ribs are prestressed so that stresses opposite to those originating from its own weight are produced. Considering that rock is weak in tension, it was aptly decided to regulate the prestressing magnitude which would take advantage of the tensile arch action and at the same time, load the foundation in an optimal manner in compression for full dead load and live load.

## DESIGN

The new design for the prestressed steel arch bridge is shown in Fig.9.1.

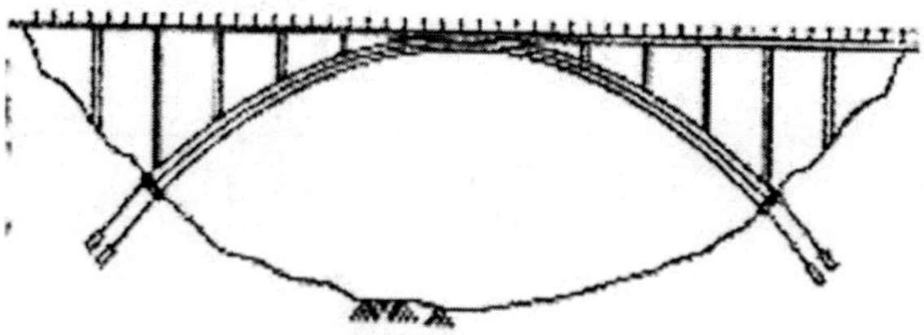

Fig.9.1

The main ach ribs are fabricated from structural steel and have a parabolic profile. The arch ribs are anchored to the rock face by prestressing rock anchors. The arch ribs are tensioned by pushing upwards using Fressi flat jacks placed on temporary towers. In the new design a parabolic arch profile was selected as this results in an economical structure for loading which is predominantly uniformly distributed. The arch rib was prestressed in a manner so as to induce predominantly tensile stresses throughout the arch section. As seen from Fig 9.2, the arch can be visualized as a tensile arch tensioned by a prestressing force P which is equivalent to loading the arch by a uniformly distributed load q, taken as half the self weight of the arch.

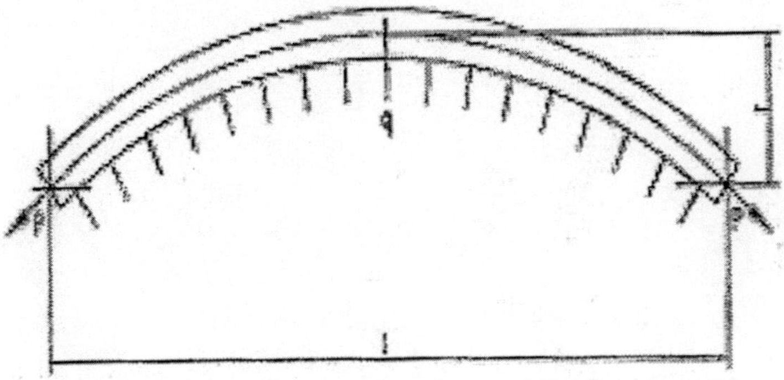

Fig.9.2

In the final stage when the structure is designed as a conventional arch under uniform dead load and live load, it resists the load predominantly by compression in the member as shown in Fig.9.3. The stresses in the structure are opposite in nature to those produced by prestress. Thus, at the final stage the structure is effectively designed for only half the dead load and full live load. Briefly the main stages of construction comprise: (a) laying out the bridge; (b) installing the prestressing bar anchors in position; (c) constructing the concrete foundation; (d) fabricating steel arch ribs; (e) erecting segments of steel arch ribs with towers as temporary support; (f) welding of segments; (g) securing arches to foundation with high tensile prestressing bar anchors; (h) stressing arch rib by Fressi flat jacks placed on towers; (i) grouting space created between base plate and concrete foundation by elongation of prestressng bars; (j) Erecting bracing between two arch ribs; (k) removing of temporary towers; (l) erecting steel portals on arch ribs to support concrete deck; (m) casting concrete deck (n) installing railings etc.; (o) conducting load tests.

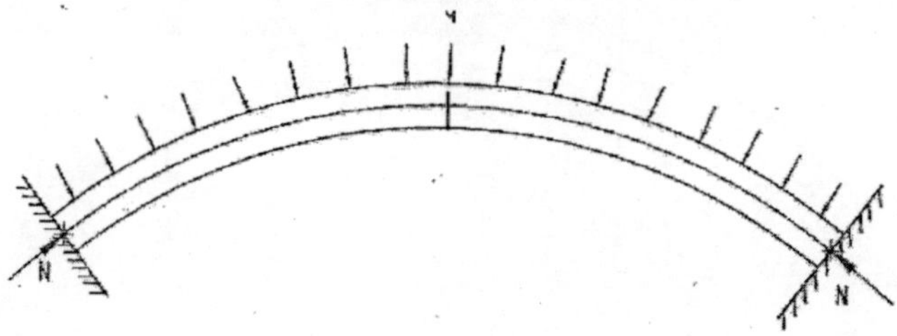


Fig 9.3

## ADVANTAGES

- Prestressing of structural steel increases the strength of the structure leading to a more economical design.
- Slender arch rib elements lead to significant advantages in handling and transportation.
- Reduced depth of structure for comparable spans, thereby reducing approach roadway costs for the large number of overpasses.
- Lighter structure reducing the inertia effects induced by seismic events.
- Greater economies can be achieved when design is used with high strength weather resistant steels.
- The bridge has exceptional grace and beauty and neatly expresses its function.

❐

# Chapter 10

## *Optimizing Stadium Capacity – A Novel Approach*

Optimizing the seating capacity of a stadium within the boundaries of the site available, continues to present an enormous challenge to the designers. This has prompted a new type of stadium design having an inspirational seating arrangement Nazir (2003). Here, an additional seating tier is added, which unlike in conventional tiers, increases in height towards the pitch and is suspended from the roof structure.

### OVERALL CONCEPT

Increasing the seating capacity is achieved through the addition of tiers. Continuing logically to add parallel rows, the boundary of maximum viewing distance is reached. Also, the depth of these tiers stemming from there required capacity generates significant height. Thus, there is a need for a stadium that would permit optimum seating within the limitations of the space available, yet keeping spectators close to the action on the field. The best place to add seats to increase the capacity within the maximum viewing distance is, by utilizing the space above the normal tiers. Fig.10.1 shows a stadium with the new conceptualized seating arrangement in which the spectators are kept close to the action on the field.

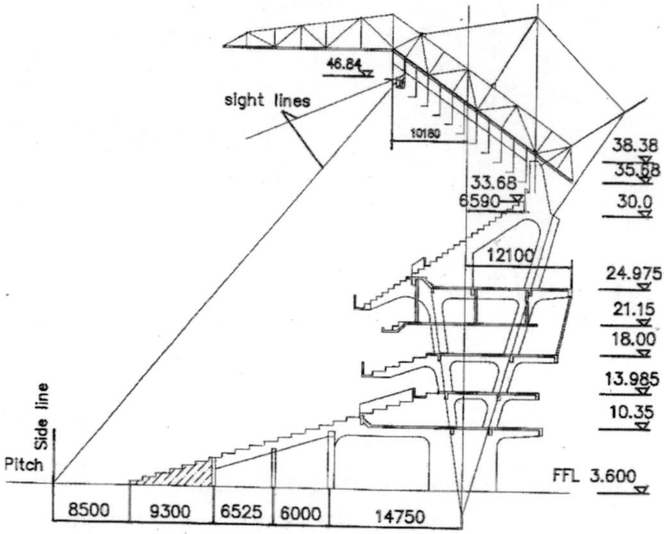


Fig 10.1

## DESIGN

The design incorporates — (a) accommodation of all major field events and (b) creation of the best possible spectator experience and spectator line of sight in comparison with the best international facilities. Once the seating numbers are decided, the geometry of the seating bowl is governed by; (a) maximum viewing distance which has to be approximately 190 meters based on the ability of the average eye to discern sports important objects; (b) each person's sight line to the nearest point of interest is determined by a viewing standard 'C' value, which is the distance between the eye-level and the top of the head of the person in front. A value of 'C' equal to 60 mm is internationally accepted base viewing standard for large stadia; and (c) the viewing tiers so generated need to be at an angle not exceeding 34° and governed by safety and vertigo. Keeping the fist line of seats at a reasonably consistent distance from the edge of the pitch and continuing logically to add parallel rows, the boundary of maximum viewing distance is reached. Increasing spectator capacity is then achieved by the introduction of a new tier raking upwards towards the pitch with the geometric requirements of the seating deck determined by the sightline requirement optimized to give each seat the best possible view. In developing sightlines, the following factors were considered; (a) for a seated person of average height, his line of sight is assumed to be at 1120mm from top of tread. (b) for objects located on the far side of the pitch, each person's sight line to the nearest point of interest needs to be at least 90 mm below the corner of the tread in front (Fig.10. 2); (c) similarly for objects located on near side of pitch, the sight line has to be at least 90 mm above the corner of the tread where the person is seated on and the maximum vertical angle ϕ, should not be greater than 52° (Fig.10.3).

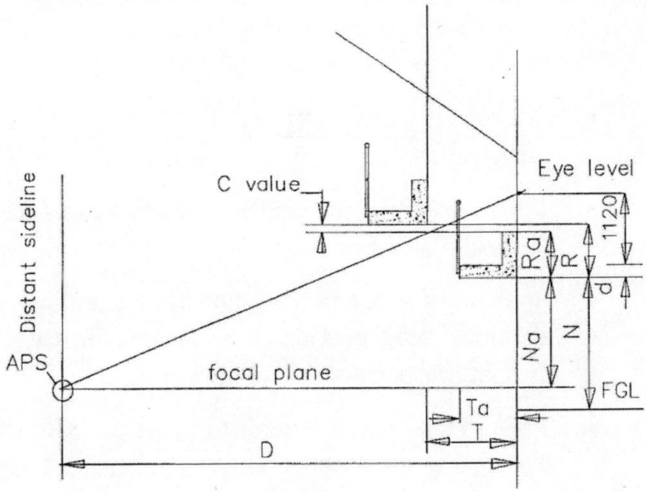


Fig.10.2

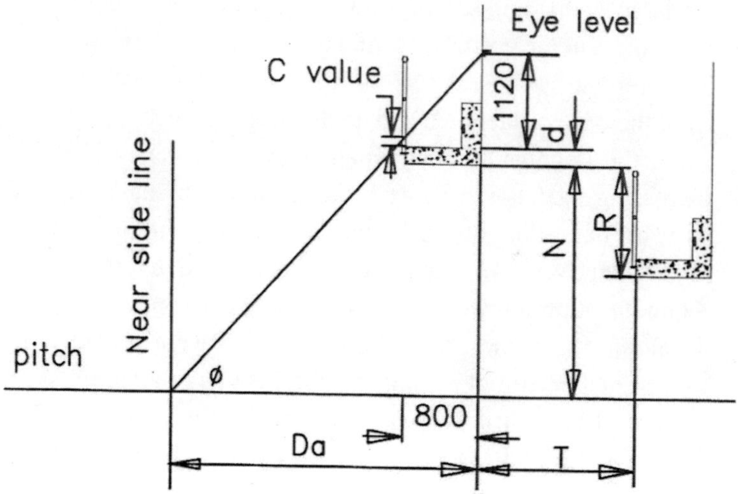


Fig.10.3

## ADVANTAGES

- There is significant increase in spectator capacity leading to increased revenues which could go a long way in funding the capital cost of the stadium.
- Additional seats will allow for wider audience participation.
- The new seating arrangement brings spectators closer to the field of action.
- As the roof structure also supports the seating tier, the additional load provides a significant increase in the damping capacity of the roof system.
- The design can be used to upgrade and increase the seating capacity of existing stadiums within the boundaries of the available site.
- Design particularly favours seating arrangement at the

end of long sides of the stadium, where the boundary of maximum viewing distance is first reached.

- The overall impact of the roof and tier design creates a dramatic skyline element. The soaring elements of the tier and roof enhance and mirror the excitement level and anticipation of events.

❐

# Chapter 11

## Reverse Jet Energy Dissipator

Water discharging from the spillway of a dam usually falls with slight resistance through the height corresponding to the difference of headwater and tailwater elevations and thus the static head is converted to kinetic energy. This energy manifests itself in high velocities which if impeded result in high pressures. When serious erosion to the streambed has to be avoided, the high energy of the flow must be dissipated before the discharge is returned to the stream channel. In conventional energy dissipating devices such as rock basins, hydraulic jump basins, baffle basins, ski jumps and flip buckets, the surplus energy is sought to be destroyed after the spillway flow has travelled through the full height from the crest to the downstream level. With rapid increase in height of dams, various problems have arisen due to erosion of scour holes and other damage involving extensive repair (see Fig.11.1) This has prompted a design for a new type of energy dissipator called the reverse jet energy dissipator Nazir (1989), which seeks to destroy the energy of the spillway flow before it reaches the basin bottom.

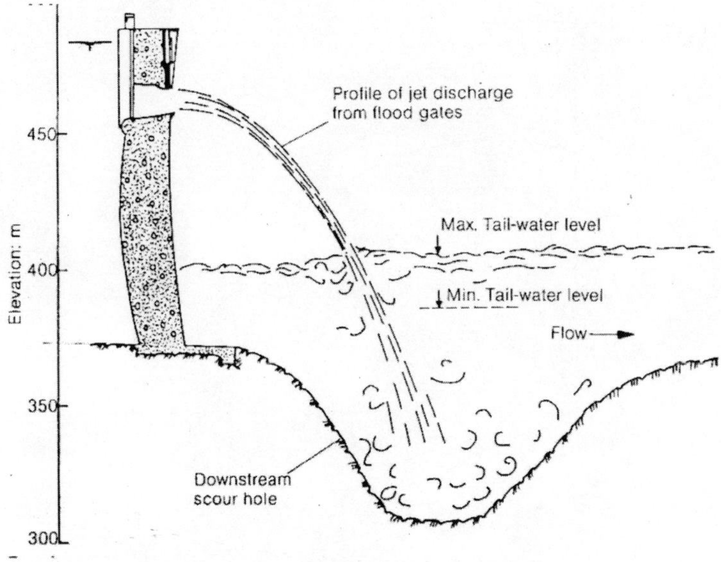


**Fig.11.1**

## OVERALL CONCEPT

The present concept was developed along lines similar to that employed for interacting jet dissipators, where the supercritical flow is split into a pair of horizontal jets which move in opposite direction to have direct impingement for energy dissipation. Here, the object being to utilize the energy of the free falling stream to drive a column of water at high velocity through a specially designed pipe (see Fig 11.2) The emerging jet is trained to strike the spillway discharge. The resulting impingement causes an exchange of momentum which leads to a reduction in the velocity of water striking the plunge pool. This has a significant impact on the pressures experienced in the plunge pool basin, as disintegrated aerated jets produce much smaller mean pressures than intact non aerated jets.

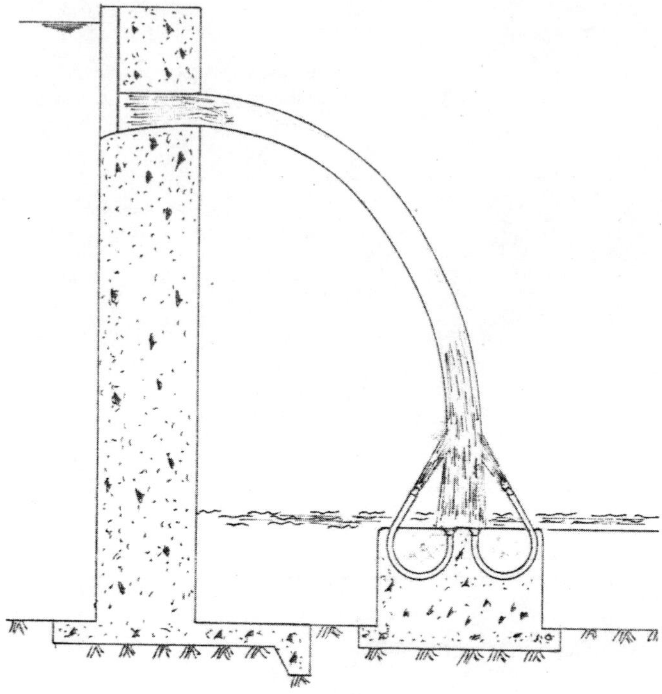

Fig.11.2

## DESIGN

The reverse jet energy dissipater essentially consists of a number of specially designed pipes, each pipe consisting of three sections: an entry portion comprising a funnel shape merging into a circular pipe of sufficient length in which the water runs full; a semicircular section of smooth radius which changes the direction of flow; and, an exit section fitted with a nozzle (see Fig.11.3). These pipes are located on the downstream face of the dam and are embedded in a block of reinforced concrete with their entry ends approximately in level with the minimum tailwater datum. Once the geometry of the falling jet is established for the various rates of flow, the zone of flow establishment is calculated. The entry point of the reverse jet dissipater is located within this zone. Making an assumption that the nozzle jet of diameter $d$ will have a zone of influence of $2d$ on the falling nappe, the number of pipes required are determined.

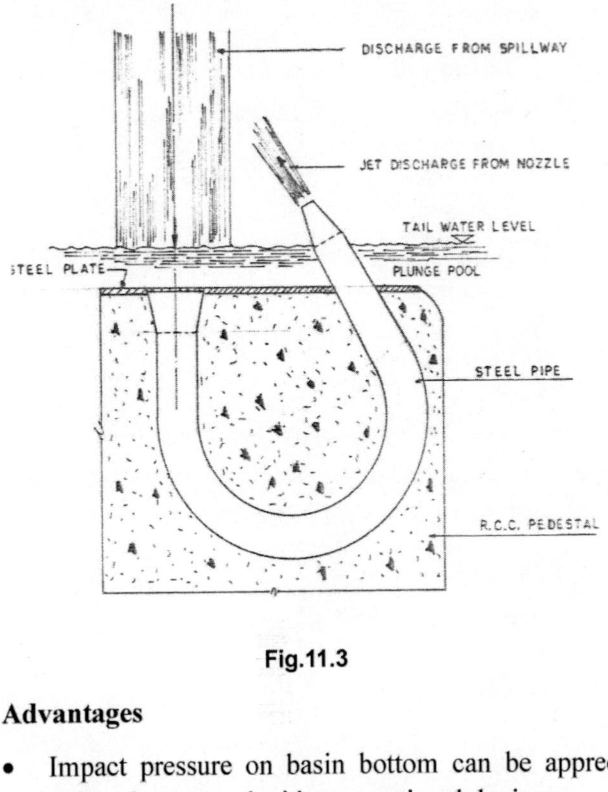


Fig.11.3

**Advantages**

- Impact pressure on basin bottom can be appreciably reduced compared with conventional devices.
- It is more economical to install than conventional devices.
- It is entirely safe in its operation.
- The most distinguishing feature of the system is self priming and it does not require any external source of power.

- It has no moving parts and is, therefore, comparatively maintenance free.
- By suitably altering pipe size and nozzle diameter, the device can be adapted to suit varying heads of falling water.
- Efficiency of dissipator improves with increase in height of head.

❐

# Chapter 12

# The Launch Rotator – A Reusable Satellite Launch System

Satellite technology is now common place and is used for a wide range of applications – ranging from direct broadcast to signal distribution and tracking, weather forecasting etc. Launching a satellite calls for a propellant such as a rocket which can move it high enough and fast enough to make it orbit the earth at constant height indefinitely. The trouble with conventional rocketry is that the propellant dwarfs the satellite, so most of the rockets thrust are used to simply move its own fuel. Further, the rockets and fuel tanks are lost in space. A major saving in the cost is, therefore possible if the hardware is to be used repeatedly. This has prompted in proposing a novel launch system called the launch rotator, which is a reusable low cost earth- to-low orbit launch system Nazir (2005).

## OVERALL CONCEPT

Imagine a bullet fired from a gun. The gravity pulls the bullet down towards the earth. If a bullet can be fired with sufficient force, then it would never reach the ground , rather the bullet will be in orbit. The idea behind the new concept is similar, except that centrifugal force is used to sling the vehicle into orbit. In the new concept the satellite rides on the end of an arm, which rotates about its centre of mass and accelerates the satellite to the orbital velocity. The idea is to store up a lot of energy by spinning the arm (rotator). Then, that energy is released to hurl a probe from earth towards space, eliminating the need of a booster rocket.

## DESIGN

The design was aimed at imparting sufficient kinetic energy to the payload, so that it can overcome the gravitational binding force to escape the earth's gravitational field. The new design is shown in Fig.12.1. It has a rotating arm having two spans of unequal length, which revolves on an axle supported on two bearing blocks with a brake. Two rocket engines are mounted on the arm to provide rotary motion. The payload comprising the satellite with its final stage rocket motor is enclosed in a heat shield and docked at the extreme end of the longer portion of the arm. A counterweight is attached to the shorter portion of the arm, so as to balance the centripetal forces developed during the rotation of the arm. The whole assembly is mounted in a pit. The first design requirement is to establish the vertical speed required to launch the payload, given the basic parameters such as weight of payload, type of orbit, height and velocity at which final stage rocket to be ignited. The size of rocket engines, their thrust, burn time and location on arm are evaluated to give the torque required to produce the rotation. Similarly, the size of rocket motor to place the satellite in precise orbit is calculated. The time of release of payload to coincide with payload having reached its angular speed and when it is in an horizontal plane. The energy imparted to the payload should then enable it to climb vertically without any external thrust. The pit is constructed in heat resistant reinforced concrete with a suitable thermal protection system provided on the inner faces of he wall. Rotator arm is the most important element of the launch system. During rotation it is subjected to very high tensile and bending forces due to centripetal action. At present, the material most suited for fabricating the arm would be one having high strength to weight ratio such as plastic fiber PBO. This material has a tensile strength of 5.8 GPA and a density of 1850 kg/cum.

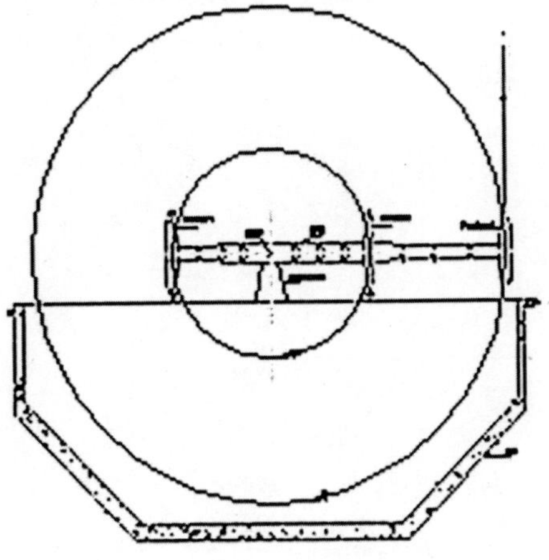

Fig.12.1

## ADVANTAGES

- The use of rockets to overcome the force of gravity is utilized much more efficiently by combining it with a boost from centripetal force.
- Expense of launch is reduced with main rockets being fully recoverable.
- Size of main rockets is reduced leading to ease of handling and transportation.
- The system enables the booster rocket with the prescribed payload to operate in a reduced drag environment as less

time is taken for booster rocket to reach its required height.

- The installation can be used to launch different satellites with minor modifications.
- The system can help in nation's missile defense initiative.
- The launch rotator could be installed on the moon, where the reduced gravity effects would allow spacecraft to be launched using far less energy and thus far more economically.

❑

# Chapter 13

# *Offshore Hydel Plant*

Energy is the key to development. Electricity leads the way as the most sought after commercial energy for domestic, agricultural, commercial and industrial applications. Conventional energy systems are heavily dependant on fossil fuels. The Kyoto Protocol of 1997 has led to the acceptance of most of the world's developed countries to a commitment of 5.2% reduction in $CO_2$ emissions by 2010. This transition towards a sustainable energy system will require the development and deployment of new and improved energy technologies.

The ocean provides an enormous potential as a source of renewable energy. Several types of ocean energy sources with different origins exist. The major types developed are based on wave and tidal energy. Their inability to provide reliable electricity prevent these schemes from becoming the mainstay of any generation mix. The new technology developed is called the Ocean Hydel Plant Nazir (2007). It offers a leading cutting edge technology which generates electricity in a reliable, non-polluting and cost effective way.

## OVERALL CONCEPT

In the present concept, a powerhouse structure is built below the sea level. The surrounding water forms a perfect basin to store potential energy which is released when a head is generated by a difference in water level at the turbine inlet. Water flowing through the turbine is diverted by a draft tube and led into a tail race sump. The desired level of the tail race is maintained by pumping water back into the sea using Airlift/Geyser pumps. These pumps require much less power than centrifugal pumps, but to be efficient, they need to be installed at considerable depth below the tail race level. For this, advantage is taken of the depth of sea available. The energy produced is conveyed to the mainland through high voltage submerged cables.

## DESIGN

A typical section of the new design is shown in Fig.13.1.and a cross sectional plan in Fig.13 2.

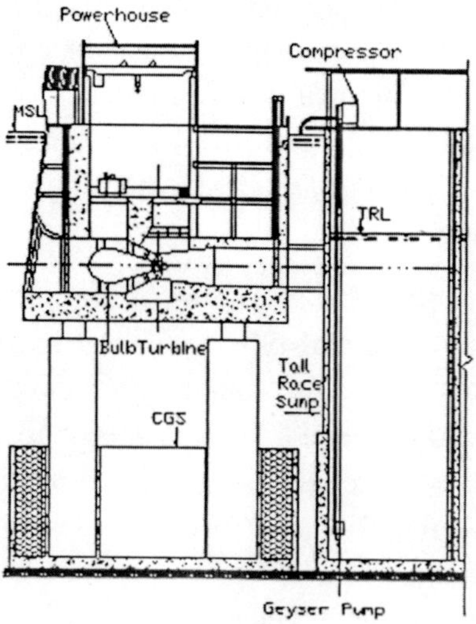


Fig.13.1

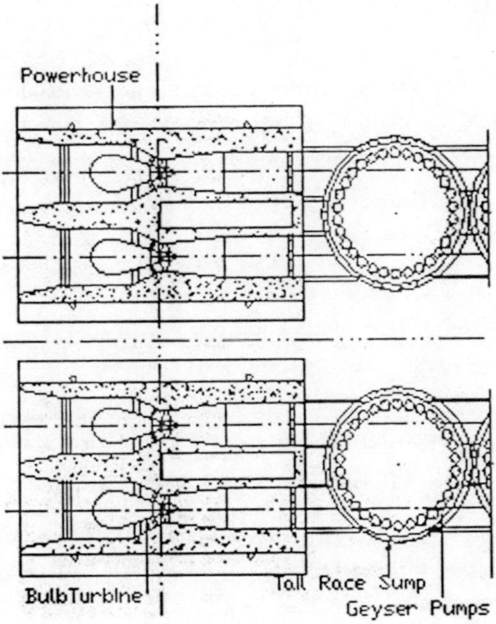


**Fig.13.2**

It has the following salient features:

- Powerhouse building comprising a turbine hall having turbines placed at a suitable depth below the mean sea level and an auxiliary bay for the cables, switch gear etc. The powerhouse structure being supported on a concrete gravity substructure.
- An intake structure to control the flow of water.
- A conical daft tube to lead water away from the turbines.
- A deep tail race sump in which are installed the Geyser pumps.
- Submarine cables to transmit the power to the shore based grid.

The preliminary design may be divided into the following stages:

- Given the basic parameters such as availability of head and depth of sea adjacent to coastlines and places of power shortage, The first requirement is to establish the estimation of power to be generated and the number of units.
- Collecting field information in the areas of climatology, seismicity, hydrological surveys, geotechnical surveys, wave modelling studies, tidal and current circulation studies, nautical studies, location of source of construction material and location of construction facilities preferably with marine experience.
- Selection of type of hydraulic turbine depending on specific speed, rotational speed, efficiency, overall cost, number of units and head.
- Selection of Geyser pumps depending on number of units, capacity, submergence level, delivery head, air flow requirement and size of compressors.
- Finalizing size of powerhouse depending on number of turbines/generators, depth of intake, depth of draft tube, number of transformers and size of cable vault.
- Determining type and size of foundation for powerhouse caisson.
- Determining size of tail race sump depending on quantity of discharge from turbines, head to be maintained, depth of submergence of pump, and number of pumps with their corresponding compressors.
- Determining section properties for the powerhouse structure, concrete gravity substructure, raft, walls,

foundation for turbo-generators, columns, crane girders, intake structure, roof structure, bed protection etc.

- Determining mode of transport and installation of offshore structure.
- Determining size of submarine cable and mode of installation.

## ADVANTAGES

- The OHP captures the potential energy of the ocean in a simple and cost effective manner. Better yet that fuel is free.
- Essentially unlimited quantities of renewable energy close to the centres of population and industry. Since the plant uses no fuel, there are no costs of transport, storage handling or the uncertainties of fuel pricing.
- Non- polluting and safe energy—no toxic gases, acids or greenhouse effects and no waste disposal problems.
- Reduces dependency on other countries for conventional fuel.
- More environment friendly than conventional hydro-electric plants: by not entailing setting up of large dams — requiring colossal funds for investment — and being associated with problems of deforestation, submergence or rehabilitation ; least impact on flora and fauna and biodiversity; and no chance of interference with transport of sediment by the dam.
- For conventional fuel based plants, the foot-print of the plant superstructure, surrounding grounds and additional facilities such as fuel unloading areas, waste settling ponds etc. can occupy up to 5 sq km of expensive real estate for a 500 MW plant. A comparable OHP would

occupy 1 sq km of effectively free ocean surface out of sight.

- Plant is reliable because water resources are available 24 hours a day, regardless of changing weather.
- The Geyser pumps deployed for pumping water have no moving parts or valves and raise more water for a given diameter than any other pump.
- An aggregation of such plants placed along the coastline, cost-effectively supplements the national electric grids of that country.

❐

# Chapter 14

# Prestressed Concrete Box Wagon

Railway wagons are in extremely high demand in India as its economic growth accelerates and the volume of shipments of raw materials dramatically increases. Among the core consumers, BOXN wagons are required for movement of coal – for both power and steel plants. There is a huge shortage in the availability of these wagons mainly due to cost and shortage of steel. This has prompted a new type of wagon design having a prestressed concrete body fitted over an under frame of a conventional BOXN wagon Nazir (2010).

## OVERALL CONCEPT

A typical BOXN wagon is shown in Fig.14.1. It comprises:

1. A wagon body consisting of side bodies and end bodies.
2. Under-frame assembled with sub- assembly jobs i.e. center sill, bolster, cross-bar, head stock, floor plates and couplers.
3. Bogie, including components e.g. axle bearing, wheels etc.

4. Brake system, coupler and draft gear.

5. Loading and unloading system .

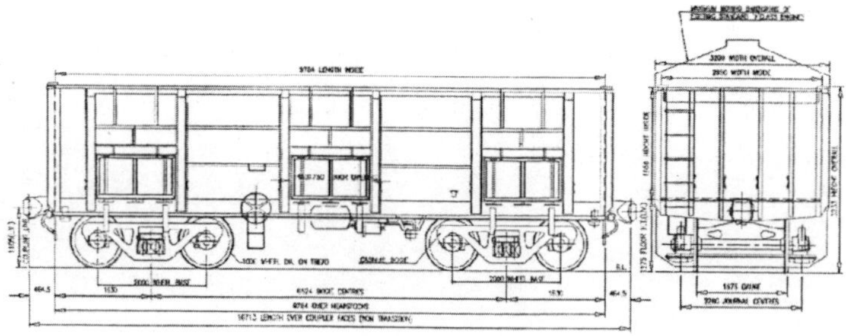

Fig.14.1

On examining the various sub- assemblies, it can be seen that the body lends itself ideally for conversion from steel to prestressed concrete on grounds of cost, corrosion, durability etc. The railways have addressed these problems to some extent by introducing BOXN-CR stainless steel wagons built with 3CR12 stainless steel and the BOXNAL wagon built with aluminum, using RDE-40 alloy. In buildings and bridges, prestressed concrete has been the material of choice when an alternative to steel structures has been sought. Thus, it became clear that a wagon body built from prestressed concrete and assembled on top of a conventional steel under frame could offer significant advantages.

## DESIGN

The new design has a prestressed concrete body attached to the underframe of a conventional broad gauge open type wagon type BOXN. This is mounted on two Casnub 22W bogies, four number 20.32t axle load wheelsets, and cartridge type bearings with adaptors, non transition centre buffer coupler and single pipe air brake system. These wagons are high sided type, heavy duty having three doors on each side of the wagon suitable for transportation of materials not susceptible to natural hazards. The inner and outer dimensions of the wagon dictated the size of the concrete/steel members. The body sides and body ends consist of prestressed concrete wall panels spanning across steel stanchions spaced as shown in Fig.14.2. The concrete is made from lightweight aggregate of grade M50 having a density of 18000N/cum. Prestressing steel consists of high tensile wires of 5 mm diameter, with strength of 1575N/sqmm. Wall panel assumed for design is 65mm thick with 23 no 5 mm diameter pre-tensioned steel placed at center of section. The stanchions are fabricated from 10mm mild steel plates and are riveted to the underframe after erection of wall panels. With this design there is a saving of approximately 3.25 t of steel per wagon.

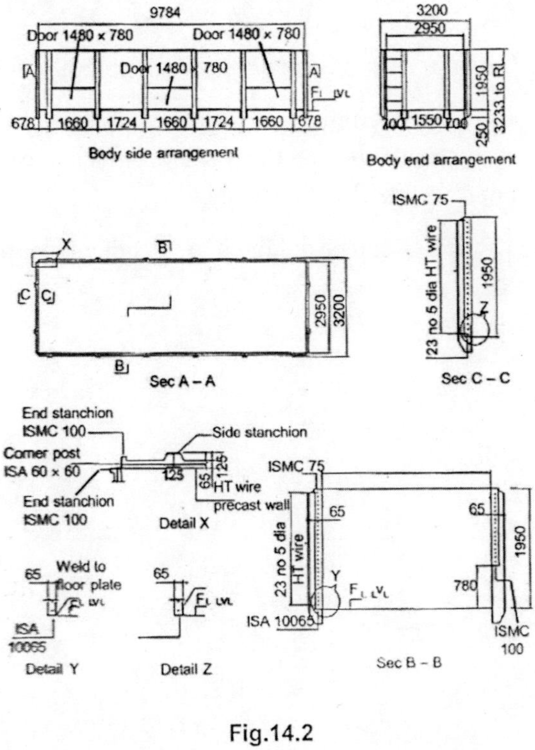


Fig.14.2

## ADVANTAGES

- The use of prestressd concrete wall panels lead to economy of material and cost.
- Steel wagons are prone to corrosion, which, in effect, leads to higher maintenance costs.
- Prestressed concrete wall panels are designed to be crack free under working load and hence no chance of corrosion of prestressing steel.
- Puncturing of panels due to improper loading is avoided.
- The new design has sufficient prestress so as not to go into reverse stress under the normal cycle range of loading and has, therefore, a reassuringly high fatigue life.
- Structure is rigid and not prone to bulging.
- Use of corrosion resistant steel conforming to IRSM for steel stanchions and other steel components can further improve the life of the wagon.
- The design can be modified to suit other types of wagons.

❒

# Chapter 15

# Three Wheel Drive Cycle Rickshaw

The bicycle rickshaw is an important mode of transport in India. It is estimated that there are over two million rickshaws on Indian roads serving eight billion passenger-km/year.. The Asian Insitute of Transport Development (1996) says that with better design and infrastructure non-motorized transport is a viable and efficient option for India. They minimize social costs like pollution and traffic snarls and are a safe and relative fast means of transport. Today, Pedal –Powered cycle-rickshaws are part of the local transport in several Asian cities, including Dhaka, Rangoon, Manila, Hanoi, Jakarta, Penang, Singapore and Macau. They have also been introduced in London, Paris, New York and Frankfurt.

## OVERALL CONCEPT

Traditional models are bulky, the aero-dynamic drag of the system is very high and they put a lot of strain on the rickshaw puller. New designs have been introduced which have aimed at making the models lighter and have gears installed to improve pedaling. Additional costs and need for frequent maintenance of gears have limited the successful implementation of these innovative designs.

## DESIGN

These have prompted a radical new design, called the 'Three Wheel Drive Cycle Rickshaw' Nazir (2003). The new technology consists of a rickshaw furnished with an additional driving mechanism operated by hand to drive front wheel so that in addition to the propulsion affected by pedals, hands transmit driving power also see Fig, 15.1. In the new arrangement hand operated cranks mounted on a short arm fixed to the handle stem, turn a large chain wheel that is connected by chain to a free wheel on the hub of the front wheel. The hand cranks are bent so as to provide a wider spacing between hand grips, which helps in steering. Also, the diameter of rotation of hand cranks and pedal cranks and the gear ratio of hand and pedal drives is kept the same. This allows the front wheel to achieve the rotational speed of the rear wheels. Further, braking comprises drum brakes. Another important feature is that unlike as in traditional rickshaws , the seating arrangement is for the two passengers to sit in tandem, see Fig. 15.2

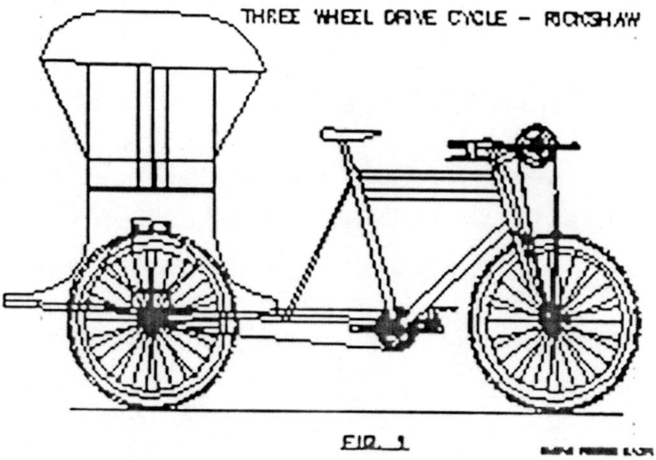


Fig. 15,1

THREE WHEEL DRIVE CYCLE - RICKSHAW

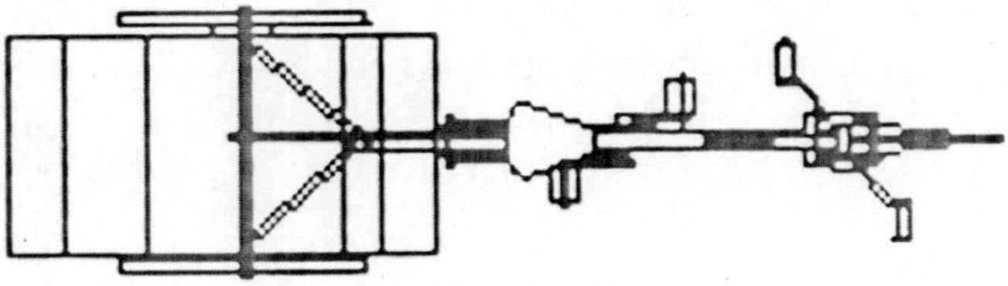

Fig 15,2

## ADVANTAGES

The efficiency of the present design is best illustrated by summarizing its advantages in the following respects:

- The new design permits synchronous movement of arms and legs which not only allows the body to function at its peak but also helps the rickshaw to generate additional torque, which translates into a greater thrusting force at the road.
- As the upper body weight of the rickshaw puller is utilized in rotating the hand cranks, the energy saved on longer trips is quite remarkable
- As frontal area is reduced, lower air resistance means less effort at the same speed; at 30 kmph the new design would require approximately 65% of the effort of a conventional rickshaw.
- The resulting narrow vehicle makes minimum impact on ambient traffic flow.
- Narrower rickshaw allows for a smaller turning circle.

- Drum brakes provide superior braking irrespective of wheel-rim or weather conditions and braking performance is on a par with cars.
- As the rickshaw puller has to lean forward when riding, the position is easier on the spine than a straight upright posture; also the glutaeous maximus, the body's largest muscle comes into play when the spine is lowered.

❐

# Part Three

## Patented Products and Technologies

"Science can amuse and fascinate us all, but it is engineering that changes the world."

**ISAAC ASIMOV**

Chapters 16 to 24 cover products and technologies where innovative solutions led to new and useful improvements for which Complete Specifications were filed to obtain patents. These include products such as bicycles, hot air balloons, concrete piles, human operated watercraft, and internal combustion engines. Technologies include soft ground tunneling.

# Chapter 16

## *Solar Powered Hot Air Balloon*

Hot air balloons are aerostats (static within the air), once a balloon is afloft, it moves in sync with the air mass in which it floats. The modern hot air balloon is made up of three main parts — the envelope, the basket, and the burner. Hot air balloons fly because the balloon and the heated air inside weigh less than the surrounding ambient air displaced by the balloon (volumetric displacement).

In conventional hot air balloons the temperature inside the balloon is raised by means of a burner using propane or some other fuel butane. The weight of the fuel to be carried reduces the lifting capacity of the hot air balloon. For this reason methods have been devised for increasing the buoyancy. A US patent No.US4174082 was issued in November1979 to Frederick Eshoo for solar powered hot air balloon, which comprised an envelope with a opaque portion and a transparent potion arranged so as to utilize solar heating to heat air within the envelope and having means to rotate the balloon during flight so as to position the translucent portion towards the sun. The main drawback of this arrangement was the additional fabric for providing translucent and opaque envelope. This added to the overall weight of the balloon as did the device for rotating the balloon, thus seriously reducing the air lifting capacity of the balloon.

Thus, it was the object of the present invention to provide a hot air balloon called the "Solar Powered Hot Air Balloon" which was an improvement on the prior art and whose performance is improved by converting the balloon from one using solely artificial means of heating the air within the balloon, to that in which the heating source is augmented by using solar energy and converting it into thermal energy to heat the air inside the balloon. Nazir (1999).

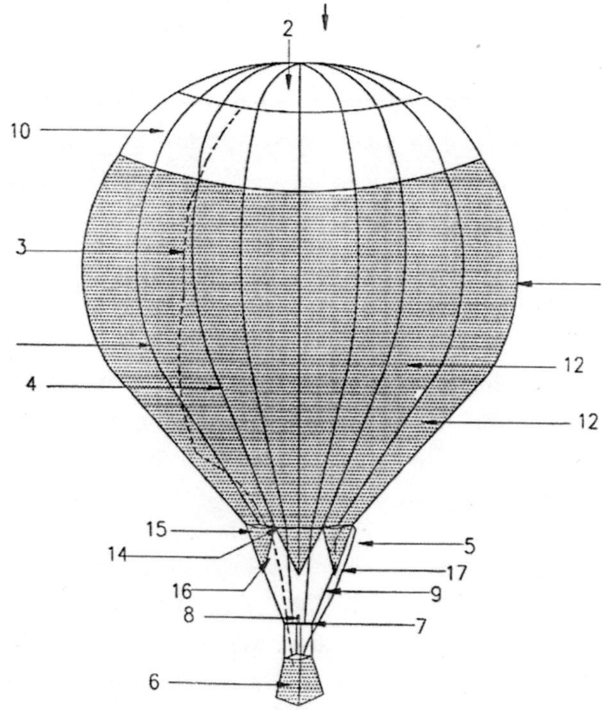


Fig.!6.1

## DESCRIPTION

Referring to the drawings, Fig.16.1 illustrates a solar powered hot air balloon which substantially includes an envelope, a parachute top, a rip chord, webbing, a skirt, a basket, a load plate, burner and suspension lines. The envelope is designed as a heat trap to convert solar energy into thermal energy with the top portion of the envelope being fabricated from transparent rip-stop nylon and the side of the envelope fabricated from a dark colored nylon with the inner surfaces coated from material that effectively absorbs and converts the suns rays into heat, such as black coloured polyurethane. The top of the envelope is provided with a conventional parachute top with rip chord for controlling venting see Fig.16.2 (FIG. 2).

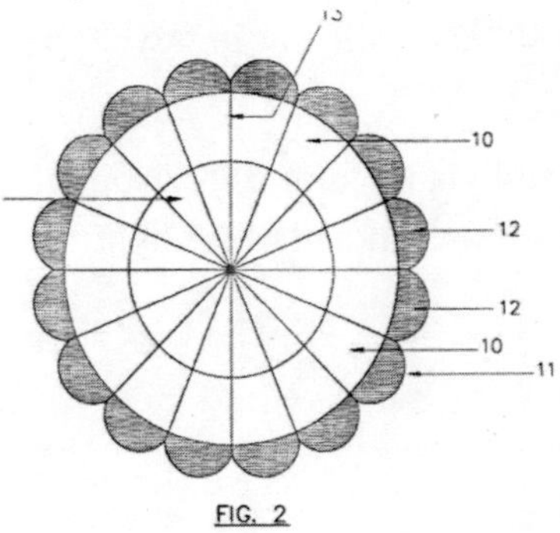


FIG. 2

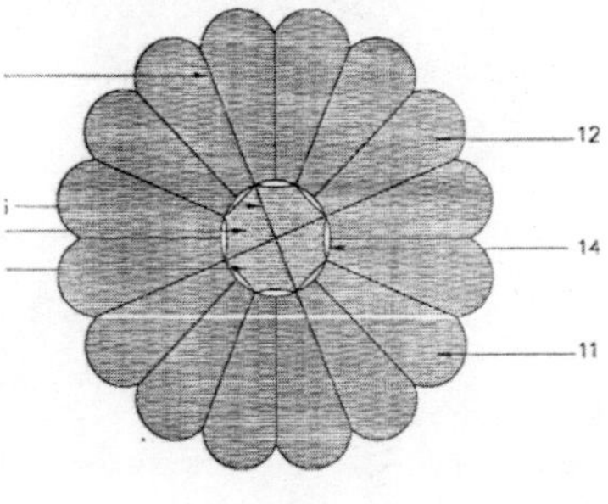


FIG. 3

**Fig.16.2**

As seen from Fig.16.2 (FIG. 3), the bottom of the envelope is provided with a skirt made from triangular panels which can be rotated upwards to close the mouth. These panels are closed when the heat from solar radiation is sufficient to raise the temperature of the air within the envelope to a level that can sustain buoyancy, without the help from additional heat from the burners.

A basket is suspended from the envelope with a burner rigged at the top on a metal frame. The burner is provided for incipient heating of air inside the balloon Within the basket are provided propane tanks with fuel lines and a control panel for meteorology instrumentation.

## ADVANTAGES:

- As the balloon uses solar energy to heat the air inside the envelope, the use of L.P.G. such as butane/propane is minimized. This makes it more economical to operate.
- With less fuel load required, additional payload in the form of passengers or cargo can be carried.
- As the mouth of the balloon can be closed, after the incipient stage, the efficiency is improved as the heat loss is minimized.
- Since solar energy is used, the balloon can travel longer distances
- It could form a cheap and viable form of transportation in areas where there is a good amount of sunlight.

❒

# Chapter 17

## *Bi-Powered Bicycle*

The modern version of the bicycle has remained unchanged since pedals and cranks were first introduced in 1861. The basic features of a bicycle comprise five main components. The frame holds everything together. The wheels that roll it along. The drive train describes all the parts that make the thing go, from turning sprockets through the chain and gears to the rear wheel. The handle bars and saddle that support the rider. The brakes that help stop the bike.

The bicycle is, of course, an ingenious, practical, and sustainable invention which has brought new opportunities for people in every walk of life. The technology development for the bike led directly to the motorbike and the automobile. It was the first example of modern mass-production precision mechanical engineering, and furthermore remains the most sustainable, green economical and versatile form of transport.

Though the modern bicycle is a mechanical marvel on two wheels, it has a problem in the same that it does not utilize the full energy developed by the rider. This is a serious drawback considering that the bicycle is operated by one's own power. Thus the object of the new invention was to provide a two wheel drive bicycle called the "Bi-Powered Bicycle" comprising of a conventional bicycle fitted with an additional driving mechanism operated by hand to drive the front wheel so that in addition to the propulsion affected by pedals, hands transmit driving power also. Nazir (1993).

A Indian Patent No.26271 was issued on March 1939 to R.S.Grawall for a hand operated driving means fitted on an axle mounted on the handle of the cycle and used to drive the front wheel and permit steering. This arrangement had several drawbacks viz.: a) the arms rotating the hand cranks tended to scrape the handle bar; b) the narrow distance between the hand cranks constricted breathing and made steering very difficult; (c) prompt braking was not possible unless hands were shifted to the conventional handle bar; (d) the additional weight and high centre of gravity of the device significantly affected the geometry of the bike and dynamic balancing of the vehicle and led to unstable riding conditions; (e) no mention was made of gearing of hand drive in relation to pedal drive and this could lead to skidding with both wheels tying to rotate at variable speeds.

Another Indian Patent No 35570 was issued on September 3rd 1946 to Gustave Brunel for a bicycle furnished with an additional driving mechanism operated by hand; specially by an oscillating handlebar with improvements suggested such as stopping of pedals, or back pedaling might be possible without putting the additional driving mechanism out of action. The main drawback of this invention was its complicated mechanical arrangement and difficulty of steering.

In the present circumstances, it has been the object of the present invention to provide a bicycle called the Bi Powered Bicycle which is, decidedly, an improvement on the prior art mechanical article and whose performance is improved by providing a conventional bicycle with an additional driving mechanism operated by hand (see Fig.17.1) for engendering additional driving power and also consist in improvements for steering, braking, and providing synchronous movement of arms and legs.

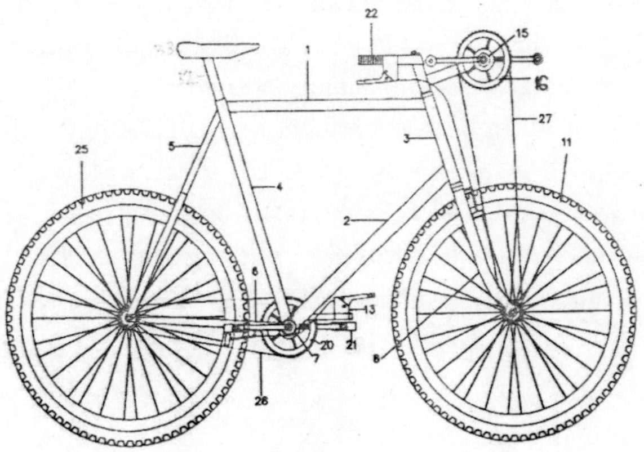


FIG. 1

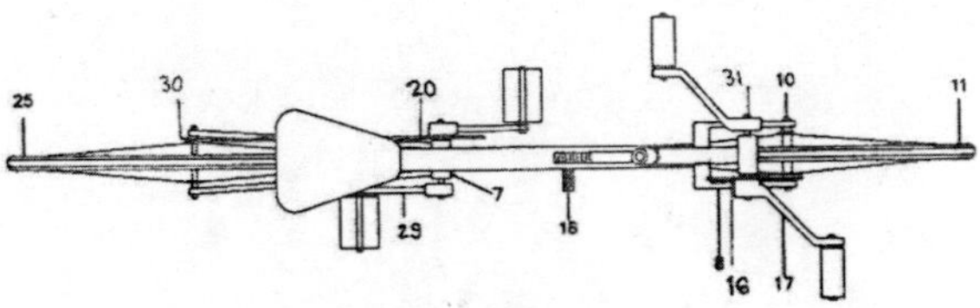


FIG. 2

Fig.17.1

## DESCRIPTION

Referring to the figures of the drawings it will be seen that the illustrated Bi Powered Bicycle includes a conventional bicycle tube frame, consisting of top tube, down tube, head tube, seat tube, bottom bracket, seat stay, chain stay, a pedal driven chain wheel drive and back wheel. Hand operated driving means to drive the front wheel connected to a front tube fixed to the handle bar system. The driving device comprising an axle fitted in a top bracket, said axle having secured to it chain wheel and bent shaped hand cranks which offer wider spacing between the hand grips for ease of steering and cranking (see Fig.17.2). The large chain wheel drive propels by chain a small free wheel secured to hub of front wheel. The diameter of rotation of hand and pedal cranks and the gear ratio of hand and pedal drives is kept same to allow for synchronous movement of arms and legs, whilst also allowing the front wheel the rotational speed of the rear wheel. Foot operated brake lever is mounted on the down tube so that rider can keep his hands free for cranking and steering. A short supplementary handle with brake lever attachment for front wheel brake is fitted on the handle bar.

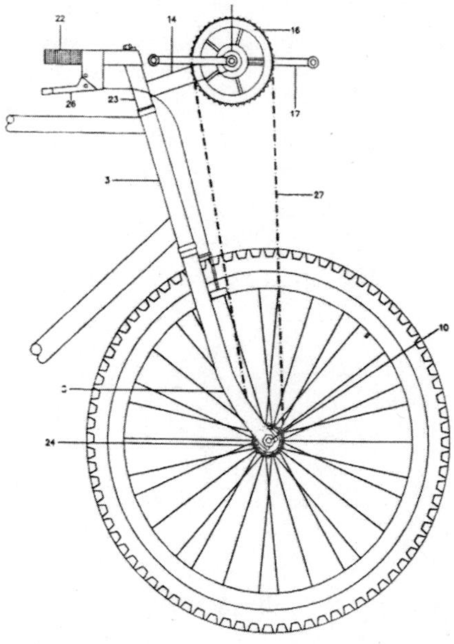

Fig.!7.2

## ADVANTAGES:

- For maximum energy utilization during the period when the vehicle is in locomotion, body physics require that both arms and legs move in unison with each other. Imagine a person running with his hands tied or a swimmer who is only using his legs. The new design permits a synchronous movement of arms and legs, which not only allow the body to function at its peak but also helps the bi-powered bicycle to generate additional torque, which translates into a greater thrusting force at the road.
- The higher torque made available ingeniously improves upon its overall performance, in respect of speed, acceleration and load carried.
- The geometry of the bike configures the body in an aerodynamic position to mitigate wind resistance for achieving higher speed.
- The rider has to lean forward when riding, and this position is easier on the spine than a straight upright posture. Also, the gluteus-maximus, the body's largest muscle comes into play when the spine is lowered. Therefore, the present invention is ergonomically designed.
- The bike is environmental friendly and would help reduce social costs like pollution and traffic snarls.
- The new product has application as a means of recreation, exercise, and as a means of sport.

❐

# Chapter 18

## Rapid Underground Tunneling Technique

Shallow tunnels for underground metro systems usually lend themselves to cut and cover construction. Most common mean of retaining sides of the excavation are soldier or sheet piles, diaphragm walls (all combined with strutting) or a composite pile to pile method. One of the greatest problems of constructing tunnels in congested cities is one of access. As an alternative for this, a new method called the 'Rapid Underground Tunneling Technique' is proposed .Nazir (1979). This system utilizes precast and in situ structural elements which are placed in an alternative sequence in trenches excavated perpendicular to the line of the tunnel (see Fig, 18.1).

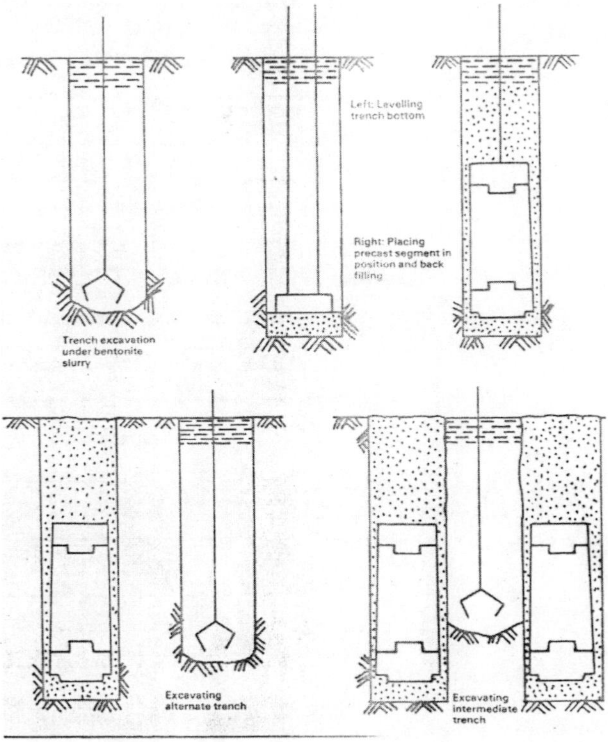


Fig.18.1

## OVERALL CONCEPT

Tunnels constructed in metros having difficult ground conditions pose serious problems as they are time consuming, disrupt the normal flow of traffic and cause settlement problems in adjacent buildings. To reduce such problems to a minimum, it was decided to have a process for the construction of a tunnel in soft ground that would limit the amount of excavation, speed up the construction work and avoid the use of diaphragm walls. The concept that developed was to have the tunnel lining made up of precast and in situ elements placed in an alternative sequence in trenches excavated perpendicular to the line of the tunnel and the elements joined in situ to provide a nearly finished tunnel at the erection stage.

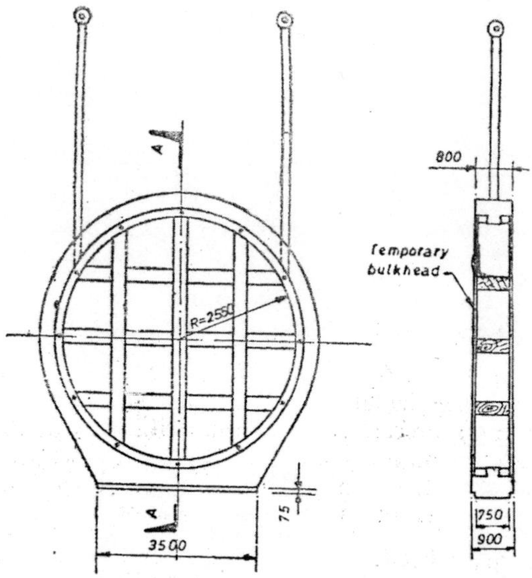


Fig.18.2

**Design** The basic design requirements should concern itself with the assessment of the stability of the tunnel and ground movements at all stages of construction. The first step in the method would be to excavate a trench perpendicular to the longitudinal axis of the tunnel. The trench would be a 1 m wide having a length slightly longer than the tunnel width and depth equal to founding level of tunnel bottom, the trench walls being stabilized with bentonite slurry. A precast structural lining element with the required internal diameter having temporary bulkheads and a steel lining on its inner face and means of connecting to adjacent elements is lowered into the trench (see Fig18.2). A further strip trench is then excavated about one ring width away and another precast ring similarly placed in position. The berm between the rings is now excavated assisted by bentonite slurry. The intermediate ring is cast in situ using tremie concrete poured around a reinforcement cage which has steel plate shuttering for the inner face only. Once the concrete has hardened, the trench is backfilled The sequence is continued up to face of destination shaft. Temporary bulkheads are removed and the segments connected by longitudinal bolts. Joints between segments are made watertight by established technique.

## ADVANTAGES

- Such a technique as described above would reduce the space required for construction.
- The application of costly diaphragm walls can be avoided.
- The use of concrete as the principal structural element would lead to substantial savings in material cost.
- Local manufacture is possible.
- Rigorous prefabrication and continuity of construction lead to an optimal reduction in construction time, thus enabling the contractor to claim release/disbursement of payment from the client (contracted).
- Ground movements could be minimized and a rigid structural lining obtained.
- As the excavation is carried out in strips, the temporary diversions of utility services need only be over a short distance and period.

❑

# Chapter 19

## *Birobic Bike*

Health, the physical, mental and chemical fitness of body determines the performance of any human being. Therefore, healthy body and mind is a pre-requisite for better performance in any profession. This has resulted in improved quality of accessories available to increase fitness levels. Stationary bikes provide an excellent aerobic activity which covers a wide range of safe, non-weight bearing exercises. They come under the category of cardio-strength machines. These machines allow pedaling as in cycling with provision to adjust resistance.

To allow maximum benefit from the workout, machines have evolved which allow movement of hands. A Indian Patent No 35570 was issued 3rd September 1946 to Gustave Brunnel which relates to bicycles and other pedal driven vehicles which are furnished with an additional driving mechanism operated by hand, especially by oscillation imparted to the handle bar, with improvements suggested that stopping of pedals might be possible without putting the additional driving mechanism out of action. The drawback of this device was that coordination of arms and legs during training did not lead to a satisfactory aerobic workout.

Thus it was the object of the present invention to provide an improved type of exercising cycle called the 'Birobic Bike' which was an improvement on the prior product and whose performance is improved upon by complimenting the conventional pedal drive with rotating hand cranks, so that simultaneous rotation of both hand and pedal cranks provide the benefit of a complete workout for both upper and lower body Nazir (1995).

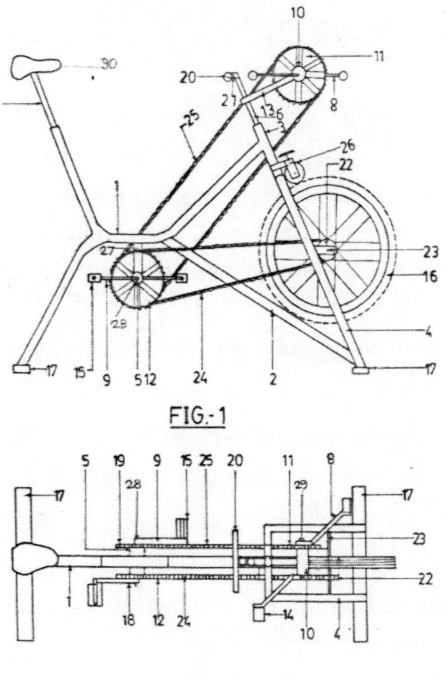


Fig.19.1

## DESCRIPTION

Referring to the drawings, Fig.19.1 illustrates a Birobic Bike which substantially includes an indoor stationary cycle built with conventional frame, stationary stand and pedal driven wheel. Hand operated drive mounted on the handle stem to rotate the front wheel. The driving means comprising an axle fitted in a top bracket, the said axle having secured to it chain wheel and bent shaped hand cranks which offer wider spacing between the hand grips for ease of cranking. The large chain wheel drives by chain a second chain wheel secured to axle of bottom bracket. The diameter of rotation of hand cranks and pedal cranks is kept same. Similarly the diameter and number of teeth for chain wheels of hand and pedal drives are kept identical. This arrangement facilitates synchronous movement of arms and legs. A short handle bar is fitted on the handle stem. A friction type speed regulator provides adjustable resistance for varied workout levels.

## ADVANTAGES

- It permits simultaneous movement of the arms and legs in a rhythmic fashion as in swimming, thus making it an ideal medium of exercise with the cycling motion exercising the lower body while the circular motion of hands firms up the upper arms, shoulders and abdominal muscles.
- The device permits independent movement of the arms and legs so that either can be exercised while the other is being rested.
- Effort required to rotate cranks can be regulated so that exercise routine can be varied from strenuous workouts to a more leisurely pace.
- The aerobic benefits are free from harmful pounding on the knees, ankles etc. as in walking or running.

❐

# Chapter 20

## Concrete Auger Pile

To keep pace with the ever-growing building industry and the many and varied foundation problems that they have generated, new and more efficient systems of piling have been developed. One particular area where demand has not yet been fully satisfied are urban zones, where piling installation require that noise, vibration and ground heave be kept to a minimum. A new pile called the Concrete Auger Pile was developed to fill this need .Nazir (1999)

### OVERALL CONCEPT

The new pile was developed to meet the general requirements of a pile suited for medium to heavy loadings, where driving through soils of soft to medium density overlying the hard founding strata, particularly in built up areas where low noise and vibration were a constraint. It was considered that all the essential requirements could be achieved by use of a pile constructed in high strength concrete, in modular lengths, being joined together during the installation process. For the pile to meet its primary function of penetrating the ground, a novel feature was introduced by developing the pile configuration along the lines of a screw with concrete bulbs shaped like trapezoidal threads formed around the shaft in a continuous helix. (see Fig.20.1).

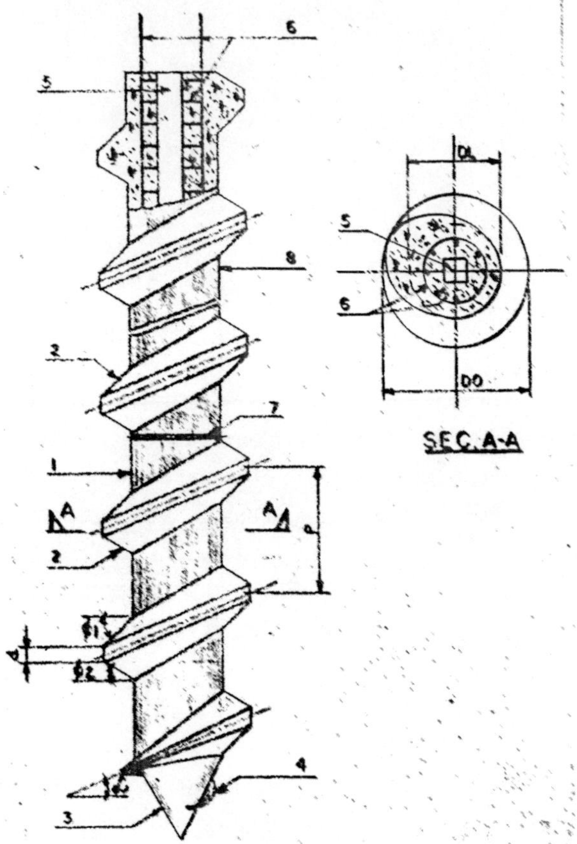


Fig.20.1

## DESIGN

The load carrying capacity of the pile depends mainly on the pile dimensions and soil strata. From practical considerations, a minimum stem diameter of 250 mm is recommended. The concrete projections which from a continuous helix around the length of the stem may be 2 to 3 times the stem diameter. A large part of the carrying capacity being obtained from skin friction along the surface area of the cylinder circumscribing the threaded projections. The pile is provided with a shoe having steel helical blades which merge with the concrete thread projections. A central hole formed in the shaft facilitates imparting of torque to drive the pile. For ease of handling piles are cast in lengths of 3.5 m, 7 m and 10 m. Steel end plates which can be welded are used to lengthen the piles. The pile is installed by means of a piling rig consisting of a heavy duty crawler mounted crane with a special mast incorporating a rotary drive table. The various stages of installation are shown in Fig 20.2 and involve: positioning the pile; inserting the Kelly bar into central hole in the pile; applying torque to screw pile into ground; lengthening using additional precast unit; joining end plates by welding and grouting finished pile.

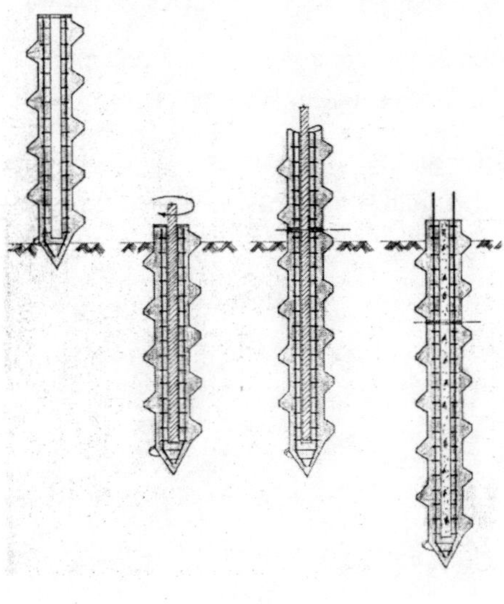

Fig.20.2

## ADVANTAGES

- In comparison with conventional piles much shorter lengths of CAP are required for similar load capacity. This leads to substantial savings in material costs beside the Management, Staff and labour costs.
- Can be installed without appreciable noise and vibration.
- Material forming the pile can be inspected for quality and soundness before driving.
- Not liable to squeezing or necking.
- Construction procedure not affected by groundwater.
- Can be designed to withstand high bending and tensile stresses.
- Can be adapted to suit installation through expansive soils or loose fills such that negative skin friction can be minimized.
- Simplicity of process allows for higher rate of installation.
- Extends the capacity of concrete piles to carry higher compressive and uplift loads.
- High quality of concrete gives increased resistance to chemical and abrasive attack and the joint is easily protected.

❐

# Chapter 21

## Prestressed Concrete Mill Housing

The choice of appropriate technology has always been a central problem in economic activity; for developing countries it has become crucial. Some sectors like heavy industry cannot do without advanced technology, but even here a closer look has to be taken to see as to how best this can be adapted to make the greatest possible use of local materials and knowledge so as to stretch the available resources to the maximum extent possible. In this context, economy in the metallurgical industry assumes special significance as industrial growth of most third world countries is tied up with setting up of new steel plants. These plants require huge amount of capital investment, most of it in valuable foreign exchange. In a steel plant, rolling mills have a vital part to play in the final shaping of steel, and their cost forms an appreciable percentage of the total cost. Hence, any reduction in the cost of the rolling mill equipment would reflect favorably on the overall plant expenditure. This has led to the development of the Prestressed Concrete Mill Housing, Nazir (1986).

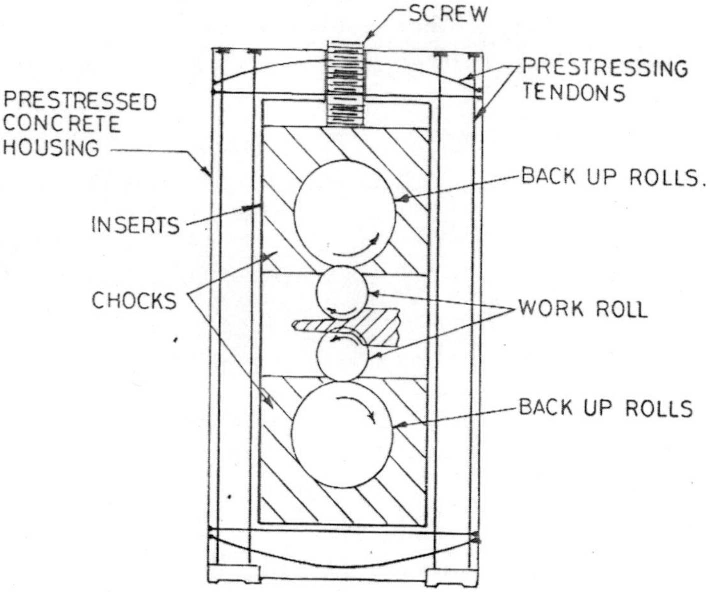


**Fig.21.1**

## OVERALL CONCEPT

A rolling mill is basically a process machine for working materials by pressure between rolls. The basic equipment of a rolling mill consists of ; (a) roll stand, (b) motor for rotating the rolls, and (c) drive mechanism from motor to rolls. The pressure of the rolls when rolling is taken by the stand housing Fig 21.1. It should therefore be very strong and rigid. Traditionally, mill housings have been built of steel. The two housings comprising the roll stand are placed side by side and connected by steel beams see Fig.21.2. It was considered that great savings could be possible if a more economical material was used in the design and construction. The innovation suggested was in the use of prestressed concrete for the design and construction of the mill housing Fig.21.2.

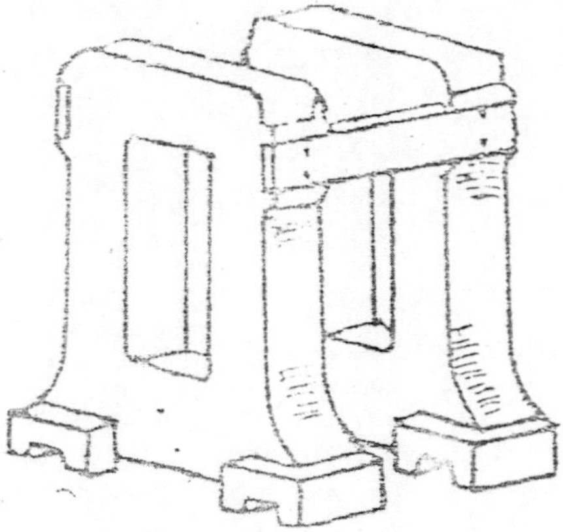

Fig. 21.2

## DESIGN

When designing a housing the size of the window is determined first. This depends on the required roll lift. The cross- sections of the cross-beams and housing posts are determined by calculation. The mill housing has to withstand not only the rolling forces, but also a tilting moment. Approach to the problem is simplified by considering the posts and cross beams of the housing of equal cross section and loaded by a force P. The resulting change of neutral axis due to bending stress is shown in Fig.21.3. While choosing permissible stresses for the prestressed concrete sections, the same factors as are applicable for steel housings should be kept in mind. Another aspect to be considered is to check if the stand is sufficiently rigid. Deformation of the housing has to be kept within allowable limits so as not to affect the quality of the rolled product. Steel inserts are provided on the concrete surface to match with the moving parts such as chocks, screw down etc. The stand should be cast in the vicinity of the location where it is to be finally erected. The mill housing is secured to the bedplate by means of bolts.

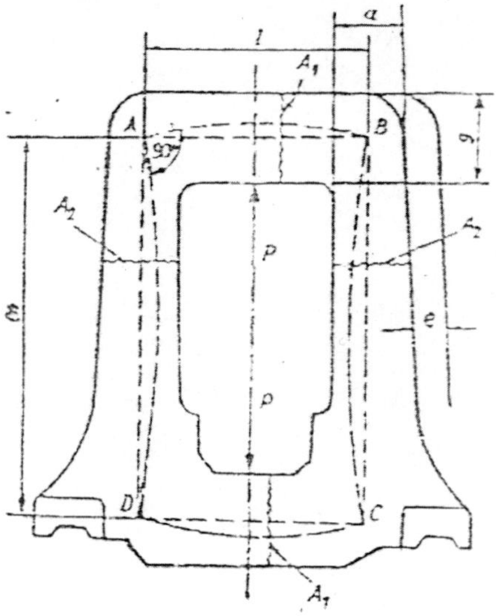


Fig.21.3

## ADVANTAGES:

- In comparison with a conventional steel housing, the elastic deformations for a prestressed concrete housing are much smaller due to the reverse camber produced during prestressing.
- The use of prestresed concrete as the principal structural element leads to a substantial saving in material cost.
- Local manufacture is possible.
- As the housing is cast on the mill floor in site, further savings in costs are achieved in transportation, handling etc.
- As the long delivery period required for supply of mill housings is eliminated, there is considerable reduction in construction time.

- A reduction in the weight of the mill housing, would mean smaller foundations, reduced crane capacities requiring lighter structures, which would all add up to bring about an appreciable saving in the overall cost of the mill building.
- Prestressed concrete has the great advantage over steel housings in relative freedom from maintenance and fire resistance.

❐

# Chapter 22

# *Manually Operated Propulsion Device For Watercraft*

Manually operated watercraft can be traced back thousands of years. These crafts have been used both for transportation and sport. Most involve rowing, a sport which attracts the third largest contingent of competitors at Olympic Games after athletics and swimming. Conventional human powered watercraft use either arms or legs to power the oars or paddles. This has two main drawbacks: (a) The reciprocating motion of the oars is less efficient in propelling a craft than the rotary motion provided by a propeller; and (b) As only arms or legs are being used, the full potential of the energy that a body can produce is not being utilized.

To overcome these drawbacks, it was the object of the present invention to provide a manually operated propulsion device for watercraft that will overcome the shortcomings of the prior art devices. More particularly it was an object of the present invention to provide a manually operated propulsion device that incorporates both hand and pedal operated cranks that can be rotated simultaneously for transmitting additional power to the watercraft, Nazir (1999)

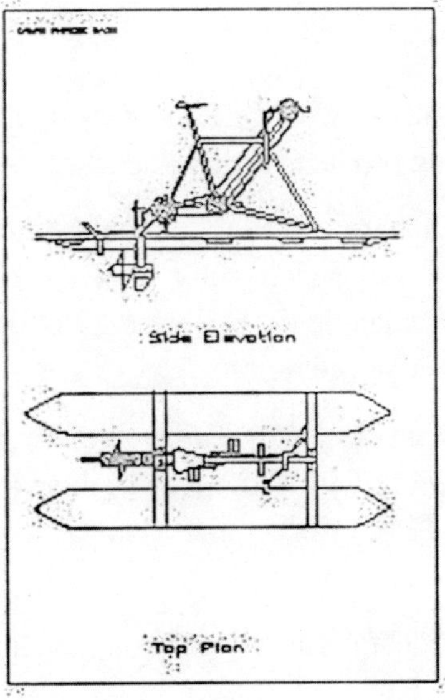


Fig.22.1

## DESCRIPTION

Referring to the drawings, Fig. 22.1 illustrates a manually operated propulsion device for watercraft comprising a bicycle type frame having attached to it a pedal driven chain wheel drive connected by chain to a hand operated chain wheel drive mounted on front of the frame. On the rear of the frame is fitted an axle having a bevel gear, which, in turn, is connected by chain to a propeller shaft on which is mounted the propeller. The propeller shaft and its bearing are housed in a hollow streamlined strut which is attached to the frame. A rudder is attached to the rear of the frame and has controlling wires connected to a lever. A short handle is fixed to the handle stem. The frame has front feet and rear feet by means of which the whole assembly can be connected by bolts to two hulls/pontoons joined together in a catamaran type configuration. The watercraft can now be powered by rotating both the arm and pedal cranks, thus turning the propeller.

## ADVANTAGES

The benefits of this technology include significant advantages over other existing products and include:

- The high torque available through simultaneous rotation of hand and pedal cranks and the use of a propeller greatly enhances the performance of the craft in terms of speed and acceleration.
- The new design permits the natural synchronous movement of arms and legs as in swimming or running that body physics require to allow the body to function at its peak.
- The product is entirely environmental friendly.
- The new device is better, as it converts human energy into rotary motion and further into linear motion more efficiently than any other human powered vehicle on water.

❒

# Chapter 23

## Pedal Drive Mechanism For Cycles

Bicycle development can be traced from the fashion statements of the 1890's to transport for the working man and woman. It is one of the most important of human powered vehicles. It has brought love and laughter, friendship and personal freedom to many lives. H.G. Wells (1866-1946) had said , "When I see an adult on a bicycle, I have hope for the human race". As long as cyclists have had pedal driven bicycles, we have wanted to improve its efficiency. How a thing functions is often where engineers begin their quest, and no object that fails to function properly can be considered to be truly perfected.

The rotational motion used by conventional pedaled vehicles results in lost energy. The majority of the rotary pedal's drive power is developed during the downward portion of the riders foot and leg motion. Since the downward motion is constrained to the arc of a circle, energy is not transferred from the rider to the rotary pedal with maximum efficiency. There are several problems with standard bicycle drive train. A rider is able to exert maximum torque on the driving axle portion of the power stroke when one of the two crank arms extend horizontally in front of the driving axle. At this point the rider is able to apply his full weight in a direction perpendicular to the crank arm and is able to create more torque about the driving axle than is possible when the crank arm is in other positions.

A second problem with the standard bicycle drive train is that at any given time, only one of the riders two legs is in the power stroke of its cycle. Assuming that the pedals rotate at a constant rate, each of the two crank arms spends on average, only about one third of each cycle in the power stroke portion of its cycle.

Various prior art mechanism have been proposed to enable a human rider to deliver more torque to a bicycle drive system throughout a complete revolution of the bicycle pedals. Such systems include those described in US patent. No. 628184 issued to Plass which concerns a bicycle drive mechanism having a multigear transmission casing mounted in a frame which is vertically movable in the casing between the crank shaft and a second shaft. An operating rod raises or lowers the frame to the required position. US Patent No. 375467 discloses a linear drive mechanism that may be used as an alternative to the conventional crank and sprocket type rotary drive mechanism, and which provides a more efficient utilization of the force exerted by the rider. US Patent No 5419572 discloses a reciprocating drive which converts linear or elliptical reciprocating motion of the bicycle pedals to rotary motion of the spindle and wheel.

None of the known transmission assemblies, however, provides the broad range of power needed for recreational and competitive cycling. Further, the complicated arrangements of such devices have limited their practical and commercial value. Thus, it was the object of the present invention to provide a pedal drive mechanism for a bicycle that employs the mechanical advantage provided by a two pulley system to increase the power output to the driven wheel, Nazir (2005). More particularly, the invention relates to a pedal drive mechanism incorporating reciprocating linear motion interacting with a two pulley system to provide greater rotational torque to the drive shaft on the downward stroke of each pedal for powering bicycles and the like.

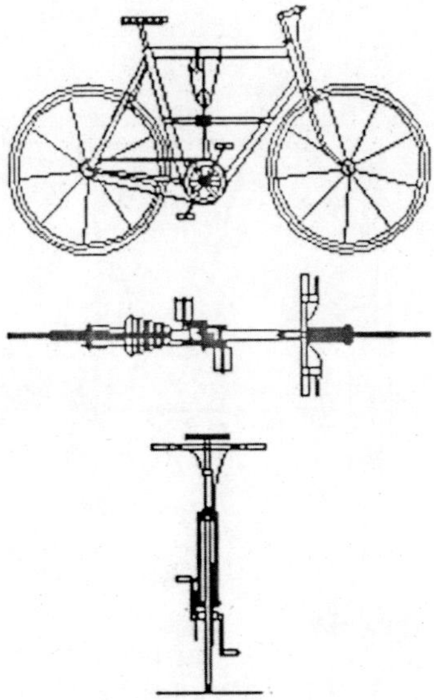

Fig. 23.1

## DESCRIPTION

Referring to the drawings, Figs 23.1 shows a bicycle with a pedal drive mechanism for imparting additional torque. The pedal drive mechanism comprises a transmission bracket; a crankshaft assembly; a right pedal crank with chain wheel; a left pedal crank; a right crank forming part of and extending radially away from right side of said crankshaft, a left crank forming part of and extending radially away from left side of said crankshaft. The left crank being half the size of right crank. Further, it incorporates a system for converting the rotary drive force to a rectilinear drive force, comprising a right connecting rod pivotally connected to right crank, and a left connecting rod pivotally connected to left crank. The ends of the rods are connected to crossheads which move in guides.(see Fig.23.2). The crossheads are provided with three wheels, so that movement between crosshead and guides produces rolling friction rather than sliding friction.

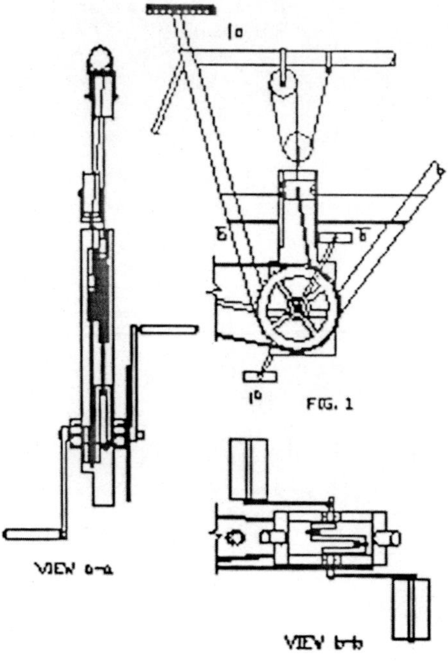

**Fig.23.2**

Yet another feature of the invention is that it includes a two pulley system comprising a fixed pulley and a movable pulley with wire ropes that interacts with the sliding mechanism to enhance the linear force. A chain engages with the chain wheel to transfer the rotation force to the rear wheel. When the bicycle with the pedal drive mechanism is designed in accordance with the present invention, driving power to the drive shaft is increased by the additional upward force on the crank. The total turning moment on the shaft is, therefore, the sum of the turning efforts on the separate cranks at that instant. This upward force is double the input force from the pedal because of the mechanical advantage provided by the two pulley systems.

## ADVANTAGES

The increased linear force is double the input force on the pedal because of the mechanical advantage provided by the two pulley system. The force is transferred back to the crankshaft as an additional upward force, thereby increasing the torque for driving the bicycle.

❐

# Chapter 24

# Improved Piston And Cylinder Liner Assembly For An Internal Combustion Engine

Internal combustion engines have been the preferred choice of prime movers for most transport vehicles. The main features of the piston engine are a cylinder, closed at its upper end and having a truly cylindrical inner surface. Sliding within the cylinder is the piston; in order to provide a gas- tight seal between piston and cylinder, a number of grooves are cut around the piston and into the grooves are sprung piston-rings, which press outwards on to the cylinder walls. The reciprocating motion of the piston is converted into rotary motion of the shaft by a crank mechanism.

The limiting factor in all reciprocating engines is the rubbing speed between the piston and cylinder wall. The piston friction depends on the pressure developed in the cylinder and the piston speed. The rings in the ring grooves on the piston, accounts for up to forty percent of power loss in the engine due to friction. Many attempts have been made to provide pistons with reduced friction.

US patent No. 6860190 defines an engine piston characterized by a circumferentially incomplete bearing skirt portion, with the thrust bearing region of greater circumferential extent than the non thrust bearing region. Thus a minimum amount of metal is used in the friction creating regions. It is also known to use lightweight carbon composite pistons described in US Patent no. 4909133, but the solution can only be met at high cost. In a further attempt to prevent metal to metal contact between the piston outer surface and the inner wall of the cylinder, US Patent No. 5901678 defines a piston having a guide ring formed of low friction polymide material.

The object of the present invention was to provide an improved piston and cylinder liner assembly that employs balls as rolling elements to transfer the reciprocating motion of the piston within the cylinder fitted with cylinder liner, so as to achieve, as far as possible, pure rolling motion without additional sliding motion associated with friction, Nazir (2009). A further object of the invention is the use of hemispherical grooves for the balls that roll within the vertical semi-cylindrical grooves in the cylinder liner and provide a rolling seal to minimize loss of gas.

## DESCRIPTION

Referring to the drawings, in Fig. 24.1 is shown an improved piston and cylinder liner assembly, comprising a piston mounted for reciprocation within a cylinder liner. The piston comprises a crown portion generated about a longitudinal piston axis and extending from the crown a substantially cylindrical main body defined by an upper annular wall and a lower annular wall or skirt. The upper annular wall has hemispherical grooves formed around the perimeter in which are mounted rolling elements in the form of balls (see Fig. 24.1). Below this is provided an oil groove in which is fitted an oil control ring. The skirt is provided with a pair of pin bosses defining a pin axis. The skirt is discontinuous at the bottom defining major thrust bearing region and minor thrust bearing region respectively, centered on the thrust axis. Three spaced rows of hemispherical grooves are provided on perimeter of skirt in which are mounted balls. Further, the cylinder liner has vertical semi- cylindrical grooves formed on its inner periphery in which the balls run. The crown has lips which are complimentary to the grooves in the cylinder liner.

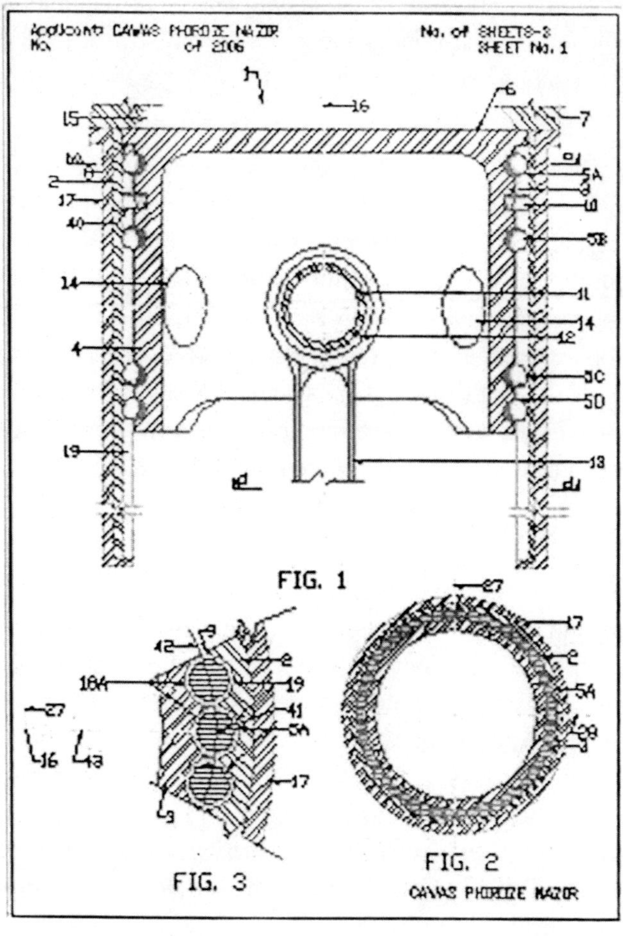


Fig.24.1

## ADVANTAGES

During operation of the internal combustion engine, the improved piston moves downwards on the combustion cycle and combustion pressure acts against the crown and the lips, the lips protect the protruding portion of the fist row of balls from the direct action of the high pressures and temperature. Due to high temperature, the thermal expansion of the piston reduces the radial clearance of the ball elements within the semi-cylindrical grooves and the hemispherical grooves respectively and together with the hydrodynamic lubrication, function as a rolling seal to maintain gas tightness of the piston. As the piston rises on the upward stoke, the lips squeeze the fuel–air mixture at high velocity out of the grooves of the cylinder liner so that good turbulence is achieved and gas pockets liable to cause detonation are eliminated. As the piston reciprocates, the ball elements reduce friction by producing rolling friction rather than sliding friction. The decreased friction allows for higher piston speeds inherently increasing the usable power. Also, the starting friction is low, a desirable feature since full flow of oil cannot occur until the engine has been started. The arrangement of balls in their deep groove bearings provide for long service life, low lubrication consumption, hardly any wear and possibility of rapid fitting and dismantling. An added advantage related to the geometry of the cylinder liner is that larger piston-swept working volume of the cylinder ( due to addition of spaces formed by the approximately semi-cylindrical grooves) allow for a larger volume of fuel- air mixture being forced into the combustion chamber thus resulting in an increase in the compression ratio. This results in better fuel utilization, an increase in effective pressure and, therefore, in engine power output.

❐

# Part Four

## Commercialising Products and Technologies

"One might think that the money value of invention constitutes its reward to the man who loves his work. But... I continue to find my greatest pleasure and so my reward in the work that precedes what the world calls success."

**Thomas A. Edison**

Chapter 25 covers the Innovation Process that describes the process of effectively planning the technical, marketing and business development of the new technology.

Chapter 26 gives the various steps in obtaining a patent.

# Chapter 25

## *From Invention To Innovation*

"A fortune awaits the man who invents even the simplest article if it serves mankind well".

Once a device is invented, the inventor has to find an application for it. This requires the conversion of that invention into business. Innovation may be described as a summation of invention and its exploitation.

### THE INNOVATION PROCESS

To get an innovation into the market you not only need to develop a technology that works. The technical development must be linked to an assessment of both your market and the channels through which you may achieve it. In addition you must evolve a business structure appropriate to your stage of technical development. A business structure must meet needs for market research, requirements for capital, regulation agencies, and the necessity to protect your investment in your technology.

This coordinated linkage of technical, market and business development of a new technology represents the " Innovation

Process". By comprehending the process you can plan effectively; unless you plan effectively you have little chance of your idea being commercialized. Tiwary (2007).has described the simplified innovation process as one that may be categorized into three broad phases (see Fig.25.1)

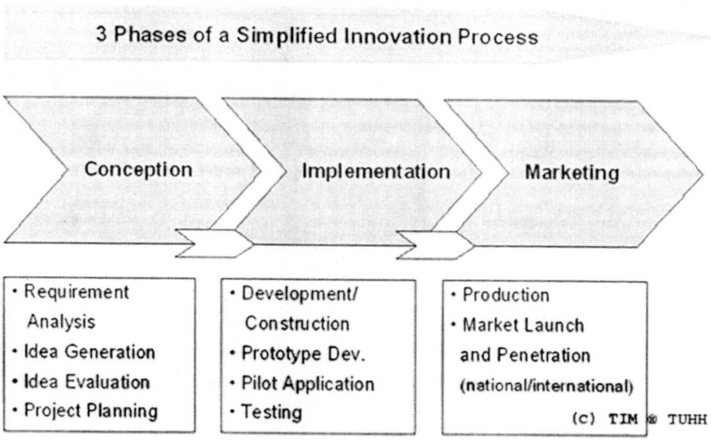


**Fig.25.1**

Systematic planning begins by planning in writing, your technical, marketing and business strategies.

While developing a new technology, however, most innovators tend to focus primarily on the invention itself: Does it work? Can it be made to work? If it works, does it do the task as well as or better than existing method? In fact, the most crucial question is not if it will work; but assuming it works, will anybody buy it. Hence, it becomes necessary to focus on the question as how and to whom you will sell your technology.

To reach the market, somebody has to produce your technology, and somebody has to sell it. Basically, there are two ways to commercialize a technology: license someone else to produce and/ or sell it, or you do the job yourself. Whether you want to market it yourself, or convince someone else to buy the rights to do it, you need to put together a convincing package. This would comprise:

*Proof that it works.* A good way to interest the investors would be to make a working model or an engineering prototype. There's not much hope of interesting would be investors if they cannot see, touch, and watch the physical object.

*Market analysis.* This would require an evaluation of who the potential customers are, how many of them there are, how much they will pay, what the competition is, and how you will beat it. You also need to know exactly what the market channels are through which products like yours reach the market.

*Commercialization plan.* This is a detailed analysis showing what you want to do to develop, market, and sell your technology, how much all this will cost, and who will do all this work required. This should be translated into a yearly statement of costs projected over a period of five years. Investors and or prospective licensees will need to see such a plan.

Before you make a substantial investment of time, money, or effort in technical development, you should have lucid, credible answers to the questions as outlined in this Invention Feasibility Checklist.

- If the device does what is intended, is there a market, ie. will anyone buy it ?
- Does it offer real BENEFITS?
- It is really novel and non-obvious?
- Does it solve a real problem?
- Is it a revolutionary improvement (or) a significant enough revolutionary improvement that it will have a market advantage over the existing technology?

- Has a patent and prior art search been conducted and is it patentable?
- Are functional alternatives to the device readily available?
- Has a prototype been built and can it be demonstrated?
- Can others make claim against the title (e.g. former employers)?
- Will customers pay a premium for the product?
- Can it be manufactured at a reasonable cost?
- Does it need regulatory approval, and how long is this expected to take?
- If you want to license it, can it be integrated into an existing product line?
- Is the current overall market category significant in terms of absolute money?
- What market share percentage can it hope to capture, and in what time period?
- Is the market growing?
- Are you willing to stick with it for years?
- Are you willing to invest your own money or is there advance backing?

You may have a business plan; you may have a patent or a license; you may have the necessary financing; but can your project be made at a cost and sell at a price that will yield enough profit to make your business profitable. Unless you are convinced about its viability, it would not be prudent to go ahead with the technical development.

If, on the other hand, you can demonstrate that your invention has strong profit potential, then you can turn you attention to the technical development steps ahead of you.

There are six major steps from concept to production:

- The Concept / Idea
- Concept Analysis
- Working Model / Proof of Concept
- Engineering Prototype
- Production Prototype
- Qualified Production Item

Bridging the gaps between these steps may be straight forward or complicated depending on the complexity of the product. Once, you have a full-scale, fully operational model you are close to getting to the brink of market entry.

For the progressive development of The Innovation Process, you will have to select a commercialization strategy for your technology. This requires systematic analysis that integrates the technical, market, and business dimensions of your project. For this you need to draw up a plan.

Your plan may begin as a simple description of your project including the technology, information on management, commercialization strategy, resources required for development, and so forth. The plan for licensing or venturing should consist of the following:

- Cover page
- Table of contents
- Executive summary
- The Project

- The Product
- The Market

Developing a plan will help you derive multiple benefits:

- It will crystallize your ideas about how you want to commercialize your technology.
- It lets you develop project management.
- It will help you develop the information necessary to convince others to consider procurement of license under your technology, or invest in it.
- It establishes an action plan to which you can refer continually.
- It helps you establish goals and performance targets.
- A completed plan may serve as a marketing tool.

Planning requires an ongoing process of information collection that supports a coordinated systematic approach to technical development, market assessment and marketing strategy as well as the assembly of an appropriate business structure. The document will take a lot of hard work but the work will eventually pay of.

It is worth remembering that research has shown that starting from a bright new idea, those that survive all the way to successful application are less than one percent. Even after that, those that survive long enough to compete for entry probably fail ninety five percent of the time.

❒

# Chapter 26

# Filing Patent Applications

## DISCLAIMER

The main purpose of this chapter is to provide basic information, it is not meant as a substitute for professional legal advice.

When an inventor has created something he feels is useful, or is something new and further he believes the public will buy, he needs to protect his idea so that he may safely negotiate with interested parties without having the fear that his idea/invention may be stolen. The method to do this is to apply for a patent.

## WHAT IS A PATENT

(With acknowledgement to Govt. Of India, The Patent Office, Kolkata).

A patent is a grant of exclusive right for limited period by the Government to the owner of the patent, in exchange of full disclosure of his invention, for making, using, selling the patented product/process or authorizing others to do so. The purpose of this system is to encourage inventions by promoting their protection and utilization so as to contribute to the development of industries, which, in turn, provide better utilities to the society.

## VARIETIES OF PATENTS

Three types of patents are granted, namely : a) Ordinary Patents; b) Patents of addition (granted for the unexpired term of the main patent); c) Convention applications with priority date, claiming on the basis of filing in Convention Countries.

## WHAT MAY BE PATENTED

Inventions are patentable. An invention means any new and useful art, process, method or manner of manufacture, machine, apparatus or substance produced by manufacture, and includes any new and useful improvement of any of them, and an alleged invention.

## WHAT IS NOT PATENTABLE

1. An invention that is frivolous or that claims anything obviously contrary to well established natural laws;
2. An invention the primary or intended use of which could be contrary to law or morality or injurious to health;
3. The discovery of a scientific principle or the formulation of an abstract theory;
4. The mere discovery of any new property or new use for a known substance or of the mere use of a known process, machine or apparatus unless such known process results in a new product or employs at least one new reactant;
5. A substance obtained by a mere admixture resulting only in the aggregation of the properties of the components thereof or a process for reducing such substance;
6. The mere arrangement or rearrangement or duplication of known devices, each functioning independently of one another in a known way;
7. A method or process of testing applicable during the process of manufacture for rendering the machine,

apparatus or other equipment more efficient, or for the improvement or restoration of the existing machine, apparatus or other equipment, or for the improvement or control or manufacture;

8. A method of agriculture or horticulture;

9. Inventions relating to atomic energy.

## GENERAL PROCEDURE FOR OBTAINING A PATENT

The following are the successive stages of the procedure for obtaining a Patent.

1. Filing an application for a patent accompanied by a provisional specification or a complete specification;

2. Filing the complete specification if a provisional specification accompanied the application;

3. Examination of the specification;

4. Acceptance of the application and advertisement of such acceptance in the official Gazette;

5. Overcoming opposition, if any, to the grant of a patent;

6. Sealing of the Patent.

## DOCUMENTS REQUIRED FOR FILING AN APPLICATION

1. Application form in triplicate.

2. Provisional or Complete Specification in triplicate.

3. Drawing in triplicate.

4. Abstract of the invention in triplicate.

5. Information and undertaking listing the number, filing date and current status of each foreign patent application in duplicate.
6. Priority document in convention application.
7. Declaration of inventorship where provisional application is followed by complete specification or in case of conventional specification.
8. Power of attorney (if filed through a Patent Agent).
9. Fee

**Provisional Specification**

It should contain the description of the invention with drawing if required. it is not necessary to include claim. However, the complete specification including fairly based on the matter disclosed in the provisional specification should be filed within 12 months of the date of filing of provisional specification. The date of patent will be the date of filing the complete specification.

**Complete Specification**

Complete specification shall fully describe the invention with drawing if required disclosing the best method known to the applicant and end with claims defining the scope of protection sought. Normally, it should contain the following matter 1) Title of invention; 2) Field of invention; 3) Background of invention with regard to the drawback of associated with known art; 4) Object of invention; 5) A summary of invention; 6) A brief description of the accompanying drawing; 7) Detailed description of the invention with reference to drawing; 8) Claims.

**Date of Patent**

Date of patent is the date when complete specification is filed.

**Duration**

A patent lasts for 20 years from the date of filing the complete specification. However, for food, drug, and insecticide patents, the life is 7 years from the date of complete specification, or 5 years from date of sealing whichever is shorter.

General Patent laws differ from country to country and they are valid only in one country. For this reason there is no "World Patent" or " International Patent." However there is an international filing system that is accessible in accordance with patent cooperation treaty (PCT) when an applicant files one of the member states of the (PCT), this is legally equivalent to filing it with all PCT member states, which have been designated in the application. Patent right is granted only by the particular member country after entering the national phase in that country.

❐

# Bibliography


## BOOKS

1. Petroski Henry 2000, *How Engineers Get from Thought to Thing*. Universities Press (India) Limited
2. Thring M.W. and Laithwaite E.R. 1977, *How to Invent*, Macmillan Press , London
3. Rawlinson J.G. 1994, *Creative Thinking and Brainstorming*. Gower Publishing Co. Pvt. Ltd. Hamshire, England.
4. de Bono, Edward, *Lateral Thinking, A Text Book of Creativity*. Ward Lock
5. Gordon, William J.J.,1961, *Synectics*. Harper and Row, New York
6. Fobes Richard,1993,*The Creative Problem Solvers Toolbox* Universities Press (India) Ltd

## PAPERS AND ARTICLES

1. Nazir, C. P., 'Multispan Balanced Suspension Bridge'

Journal of Structural Engineering A.S.C.E., USA, Nov 1986

2. Nazir, C. P., 'Ground Improvement Technique through Shock Wave Propagation', Journal of The Institution of Engineers (India) January 1981

3. Nazir, C. P., 'Concrete Auger Pile' Proceedings of the Indian Geotechnical Conference 1992

4. Nazir, C. P., 'Prestressed Concrete Rolling Mill Stand', Proceedings of 11th Conference on Our World in Concrete and Structure Singapore, August 1986

5. Nazir, C. P., 'An Earth Balanced Cantilever Bridge' , Journal of The Institution of Engineers (India) January 1984

6. Nazir, C. P., 'An Improved Design for Low Cost Housing', Journal of The Institution of Engineers (India), Sep. 1985

7. Nazir, C. P., 'Prestressed Aluminum Arch Dam' Proceedings of IABSE Symposium Rio de Janeiro, on Structures for the Future, August 1999

8. Nazir, C. P., 'Prestressed Steel Arch Bridge', Journal of The Institution of Engineers (India), May 2003

9. Nazir, C. P., ' Optimizing Stadium Capacity – a Novel Approach', Journal of The Institution of Engineers (India), October 2003

10. Nazir, C. P., 'Reverse Jet Energy Dissipator', Journal of The Institution of Engineers (India), February 1989

11. Nazir, C. P., 'Rapid Underground Tunneling Technique', Journal of The Institution of Engineers (India), January 1980

12. Nazir, C. P., ' The Launch Rotator – a Reusable Satellite Launch System', Journal of The Institution of Engineers (India), May 2005

13. Nazir, C. P., 'Offshore Hydel Plant', Submitted for Virgin Earth Challenge, March 2007

14. Nazir, C. P., 'Prestressed Concrete Box Wagon', Journal of The Institution of Engineers (India), Nov 2010

15. Nazir, C. P., Dual Drive Cycle Rickshaw Entry – National Innovation Foundation, Ahmedabad 2003

16. Thapar .K 'Current Status and Policy Issues, Nationalized Motorized Transport, Asian Institute of Transport New Delhi 1996

17. Tiwari R. et al 'Innovation via Global Route', Paper presented with Proceedings on the 2nd International Conference on Globally Distributed Work held by IIM, Bangalore July 2007

## PATENTS GRANTED AND APPLIED FOR

1. Nazir C.P. 'Improved process for the construction of tunnel in soft ground' Government of India Patent Office, Patent No.150023 issued on 14th June, 1979.
2. Nazir C.P. 'Rolling mill with stand for housing Government of India Patent Office, Patent No.154580 issued on 24th April, 1982.
3. Nazir C.P. 'Bi Powered Bicycle', Government of India Patent Office, Patent No.178767 issued on 19th April, 1993.
4. Nazir C.P. 'Birobic Bike' Government of India Patent Office, Patent No.183649 issued on 30th October, 1995.
5. Nazir C.P. 'Concrete Auger Pile', Government of India

Patent Office, Patent No. 171152 issued on 28$^{th}$ March 1999.

6. Nazir C.P. 'Solar Powered Hot Air Balloon', Government of India Patent Office, Patent Application No.560/CAL/99 filed on 18$^{th}$ June, 1999.
7. Nazir C.P 'Manually Operated Propulsion Device for Watercraft', Government of India Patent Office, Patent Application No.120/CAL/99 filed on 16$^{th}$ February, 1999
8. Nazir C.P., 'Pedal Drive Mechanism for Cycles', Government of India Patent Office, Patent Application No.490/KOL/2005 filed on 10$^{th}$ June, 2005.
9. Nazir C.P.' An Improved Piston and Cylinder Liner Assembly of an Internal Combustion Engine', Government of India Patent Office, Patent Application No.684/KOL/2006 filed on 10$^{th}$ December, 2009.

## PUBLICATIONS

'General Information for filing Patent applications', Govt. of India, The Patent Office, Kolkata

## SOURCES OF ADDITIONAL INFORMATION

Jackson K.F., 1975 *The Art of Solving Problems.* Heinmann .

Mott, Jacolyn A., 1973 *Creativity and Imagination.* Monkato, USA

Prince,G.M., 1970 *The Practice of Creativity.* Harper and Row, New York

Walter, W. Grey, 1961, *The Living Brain.* Pelican .

Emmet, E. R., 1972, *A Diversity of Puzzles.* Harper and Row.

Finch, James Kip, 1960, *The Story of Engineering.* Anchor Books, New York de Camp, L Spague, 1963 *The Ancient Engineers.* Doubleday New York.

Ley Willy, 1960, *Engineer's Dreams.* Viking New York

Petroski, Henry *Design Paradigms: Case Histories of Error and Judgment in Engineering.* University Press New York

MacLeod, Christine, *Inventing the Industrial Revolution: The English Patent System , 1660-1800.* University Press Cambridge,

Smith, Norman 1971, *A History of Dams.* Peter Davies , London.

Hopkins, H. J. 1970, *A Span of Bridges;: An Illustrated History.* Praeger New York.

Davidson, Frank P., with John Smith Cox'1993, *Macro: A Clear Vision of How Science and Technology Will Shape Our Future.* Morrow, New York

Boyle, Godfrey 'Renewable Energy: Power for a Sustainable Future' Second Edition

Kalam, A.P.J. Abdul 2004, *Wings of Fire.* Universities Press, Hyderabad

Blom, Cornelius 2002, *Design Philosophy of Concrete Linings for Tunnels in Soft Soils.* Abe Books UK

Rajput, R. K. 2005, *Internal Combustion Engines.* Laxmi Publication, New Delhi

❒

# Index

□□□